T0285851

# TENNESSEE
## IN THE
### *Victorian Era*

*James B. Jones*

THE
History
PRESS

*The only thing new in the world is the history you don't know.*
*—President Harry S. Truman*

Published by The History Press
Charleston, SC
www.historypress.com

First published 2023

Manufactured in the United States

ISBN 9781467155236

Library of Congress Control Number: 2023940716

*Notice*: The information in this book is true and complete to the best of our knowledge. It is offered without guarantee on the part of the author or The History Press. The author and The History Press disclaim all liability in connection with the use of this book.

# CONTENTS

# A HISTORY OF COMMITTEES OF SAFETY AND VIGILANCE IN WEST AND MIDDLE TENNESSEE

## *1860–1862*

*"The reign of terror of the Safety Committee has passed away forever."*

Civil War committees of vigilance, or committees of public safety, had antebellum antecedents and evolved out of slave patrols and "political clubs" during the presidential election of 1860.[1] The paranoid purpose of these extralegal committees was to stamp out invented abolitionists' cadres and Black Republican dogma by any means at their disposal. As secession loomed large, they took the law into their own hands. The activities of these committees included spying on citizens, intercepting mail, pilfering travelers' luggage and absconding with its contents, jailing, coerced enlistment in the Confederate army, the forceful expulsion of individuals and the illegal confiscation of private property. These illicit committees judged as spies those they believed were political threats to Tennessee's Confederate sovereignty. Following the Battles of Fort Donelson and Memphis, these committees and their members abruptly left with the rest of Confederate authority rather than face a revenge-minded Union citizenry empowered by the conquering federal armies.

Perhaps the first documented example of a vigilance committee—in Memphis anyway—comes from August 1857. At that time, the populace was enraged over the murder of a gambler, who met his death at the hands of another gambler. As a riot began to form, the mayor doubled the police force and moved to appoint a "committee of vigilance."[2] This vigilance committee does not appear to have been motivated by a desire to defend "Southern institutions" or to have any but fleeting temporal limits.

Committees of vigilance grew out of the minuteman organizations that were part of the Breckenridge campaign in the general election of 1860.[3] Soon after the Republican victory, on December 12, 1860, there appeared a direct connection between the minutemen and a vigilance committee. The pilot of a steamboat was discovered "tampering with a negro." An excited crowd gathered on the levee. "The Vigilance Committee of the Minute Men arrested him, and, after a trial, he was told to leave town instanter." The *Memphis Bulletin* remarked: "There has been enough of this ["negro tampering"], and we trust this will be the last instance of the kind that we shall have to refer to."[4] The committee of vigilance, a self-constituted extralegal body of men that would claim the mantle of guardians of "Southern institutions," was established in Memphis. Most likely, the pattern was replicated in other cities in the state. Only four months later, one account shows that in Memphis, days after the bombardment of Fort Sumter, the committee of vigilance was active. A Kentuckian on his way home from Texas stopped for a night in Jeffersonville, Arkansas. His comments that night to the local committee of vigilance were, they determined, tinged with abolitionism. A messenger managed to get to Memphis before him, warning the committee of public safety that a dangerous abolitionist would arrive later that day. A description was given.

No sooner had the Kentuckian left the wharf when a "blue jacket," the committee's sobriquet for the military policeman guarding the city, greeted him saying, "The Committee of Public Safety wish to see you. Come along." The committee questioned him about his home, political opinions and destination. Then the committee introduced the member of the Jeffersonville Vigilance Committee, 120 miles to the west, who had quizzed him thirty hours before. But even with this swift witness, the committee found him blameless, and after consultation, he was let go. But he didn't go far. A policeman handed him a letter from the chairman, suggesting that he enlist in the Provisional Army of Tennessee. The note strongly advised it was in his interest to volunteer: "Several members of the committee think if you do not see fit to follow this advice, you will probably stretch hemp....An infuriated mob...may hear that you came from the North." It was clearly apparent, the Kentuckian wrote, "that the military power in the city had resolved to *compel* me to *volunteer*, and in my friendlessness, I could think of no way to escape....I wrote my name and thus I *volunteered*."[5]

A meeting with a committee of vigilance is perhaps best described in a fictional account written in 1862, "The Tennessee Blacksmith," and published in *Harper's Illustrated*. In this passage, Bradley, an honest Unionist blacksmith whose shop sat by the foot of the Cumberland Mountains, was accused of helping an abolitionist flee to Kentucky. According to *Harper's Weekly*:

> [His captors] *conveyed him to a tavern half a mile distant from the [blacksmith's] shop, and he was arraigned before what was termed a vigilance committee. The committee met in a long room on the ground floor, dimly lighted by a lamp which stood upon a small table in front of the chairman. In about half an hour after Bradley's arrival, he was placed before the chairman for examination. The old man's arms were pinioned but nevertheless he cast a defiant look upon those around him.*
>
> *"Bradley, this is a grave charge against you. What have you to say?" said the chairman.*
>
> *"What authority have you to ask?" demanded the blacksmith fiercely, eyeing his interrogator.*
>
> *"The authority of the people of Tennessee," was the reply.*
>
> *"I deny it."*
>
> *"Your denials amount to nothing. You are accused of harboring an abolitionist, and the penalty of that act you know is death. What have you to say to the charge?"*
>
> *"I say that it's a base lie, and that he who utters such charges against me is an infamous scoundrel!"* [6]

Bradley's defiance may have been typical of many East Tennessee Unionists, and while they were not treated gently by Confederate sympathizers, there seems to be little tangible evidence that they were proscribed from that section of the state by committees of vigilance. Instead, most were forced out by mobs or left voluntarily and surreptitiously to join federal forces in Kentucky. A report in the April 20, 1861 *Daily Cleveland Herald* told of the "intense excitement" in Memphis following the surrender of Fort Sumter. Those who were previously for the Union were not secessionists. Fireworks exploded, orations were made and the secession flag was hoisted on top of all public buildings. The Union flag was nowhere in sight. Resolutions were passed declaring the Bluff City had seceded from the Union.

The city officers appropriated $50,000 for the use of the city, and the banks offered to cash the bonds. The officers also ordered the purchase of a building for a drill room, which was to cost $9,000. About fifteen

The Memphis Committee of Safety inspects an artist's belongings for anti-Confederate renderings. *Courtesy of TSLA, 42. Courtesy of the Tennessee State Library and Archives.*

companies of infantry and cavalry had been formed. Citizens subscribed to purchase cannon for the city from federal troops. All the spare guns had been collected—everything possible was done to resist federal authority. The vigilance committee was in its element and joined the passion, posting its own proclamation, printed in red ink, requiring all who deviated from the frenetic zeitgeist to leave the city at once. They had already forced several citizens from their homes. Terror reigned.[7]

There exists confusion about just when these committees of vigilance formed. They seemed to have either existed as part of a larger parent group or evolved out of it. At least two other committee-like groups existed as well: the Memphis Board of Safety and the Memphis Military Committee. Yet for all the activity, paranoia soon set in. The Memphis Board of Safety nervously contacted the Confederate States' secretary of war, L.P. Walker, on April 23, 1861, urgently requesting "prompt and energetic action" to stop the probable Union descent on Memphis. The belief of the Board of Safety was that the city could not defend itself.[8] That paranoia may have stimulated the growth, triumph and public acquiescence to the vigilance committee as the singular agency responsible for sheltering the city from invisible abolitionists and spies. For example, communication from the four members of the military committee with General Leonidas Polk, dated September 23, 1861, indicates concern for a cotton embargo against the North but mentioned nothing about committees of vigilance.[9]

Something can be gleaned about the relative wealth and social standing of the names most prominently associated with the Memphis Committee of Vigilance. Succinctly, they were men of wealth. The man most often mentioned as directing the committee's activities was Frazier Titus. The 1860 Federal Slave Census demonstrates that he enslaved twenty people, placing him in the top 10 percent of slave owners. Census data for Shelby County shows these men's vocations varied from "gentleman," railroad president, minister, plantation owner, contractor and merchant to banker.[10] Frazier Titus, however, was the de facto leader of the committee of vigilance and directed its activities. He and his fellows had a great deal to lose from the federal occupation of West Tennessee, and it is no wonder they reacted at the slightest suspicion to keep their holdings and, secondarily, their city safe from the feared abolitionist hordes.

There is less mystery about the formation of the Nashville Committee of Vigilance and Safety. Soon after the Confederate victory at Fort Sumter in February 1862, a meeting was held at the state capital on April 24. Two resolutions were passed at the meeting, first, to join the Confederacy, and second:

> *Resolved, that in the belligerent position where in we suddenly find ourselves, the ordinary policy regulations of this city seem to us utterly incompetent to exercise the vigilance imperative upon every community in time of war. That, therefore, we do earnestly recommend the immediate formation of a vigilance committee, invested with such enlarged powers as may give efficacy to their action, and constituted of some of our best-known citizens acting in concert with the mayor and existing authorities.*[11]

In Nashville, for which less information exists on vigilance committees than for Memphis, activities soon after the triumph at Fort Sumter must have been a great deal similar to those in the Bluff City. Mayor R.B. Cheatham worried less about abolitionist spies than he did about the breakdown of established order and issued his proclamation of April 14, 1861. All good citizens were requested to restrain their excitement and aid the authorities in preserving the peace of the city. According to his honor:

*WHEREAS, it is understood that self-constituted Committees, or Individuals on their own responsibility, have notified one or more of our Northern-born Citizens to leave Nashville; and whereas it is the determination of the City Authorities to preserve and sustain the peace and quiet of the City: This is…to notify all Persons that any complaints or suspicions against Persons of Northern birth can be lodged with me for investigation, and that everything necessary will be done. And all Persons implicated can be assured that they will be protected from unfounded rumors and stories, until properly investigated by the proper Authorities.*[12]

The mayor's word of caution only stimulated activity, leading to the formation of a vigilance committee. For example, about April 23, a young Cleveland, Ohio journeyman printer, William H.H. Ewell, told how it was he came to return home. He expressed himself as a Union man after having been warned such remarks were treasonable. His personal friends were incapable of defending him. He was deported by a nascent committee. Similar was the fate of Mr. Kelley, the editor of the *Nashville Democrat*, a Douglass-Democrat paper, who left Nashville at the same time for the same reasons. The mob threatened him and the destruction of his press if he continued his disloyal paper. Kelley was determined to stand his ground. He barricaded the offices, and the American flag was raised. An angry mob gathered, ready to lynch Kelley and burn the newspaper office. Cooler heads convinced the editor to lower the flag, and the vigilance committee occupied the office. He took the next steamboat north. No Northern man's life or property was safe in Nashville until he declared himself a secessionist, ready to blindly follow the Southern agenda.[13]

West and Middle Tennessee, much less than Nashville, were completely in the hands of the secessionists. "The idle masses and demagogues… constantly harangue the masses and the people seem to be insane on the subject of Southern rights.…They…openly proclaim, that…one Southern man can whip a dozen Northern men." The evolution of a formal committee accelerated after the sudden rush to arms throughout the North following Lincoln's call for volunteers.[14] On April 27, 1861, the Davidson County Committee of Vigilance and Safety was formed to protect the lives, property and interests of Nashville from the Northern foe.[15] The *New York Times*, however, reported that:

*In Nashville the Southern intolerants have organized and put into operation a society which is miscalled "The Committee of Safety." It is the business of these men to spy out and denounce every man or woman suspected of Union proclivities, where upon follows an edict of banishment.*[16]

Back in Memphis, the vigilance committee's Frazier Titus suggested armed companies of "our free colored men" be formed to fight the looming foe. However, the consensus held that arming "Negroes" was going too far, although such companies could best be put to work cooking and washing. "They understand that sort of work better than any boys who are called to do battle."[17] The committee of vigilance abolished worship services in Black churches. Two weeks later, it softened its edict so "that when the regular minister of a church, attended by *respectable white* persons, will agree to hold afternoon services, that the same be allowed." Having few abolitionists to police, the committee reigned in the least dangerous people among them. But the committee of safety did not restrict itself to controlling Black religious services. In mid-May, the *Louisville Journal*, by now an active critic of the Memphis Committee of Vigilance, printed a column outlining the calumnies of the committee. Two young men had decided Memphis was no longer a desirable place to do business. One of them, at the committee's prodding, was left to hide outdoors. "The other was waited upon by a Committee of Safety.…[They] informed him that if he intended to remain, he must join a military company, and if he did not, he had better leave the following morning." He decided to leave, and a ticket was purchased for him on the morning train. As he went to the train station, he saw numerous posters explaining that there were but two factions in Memphis—friends and foes—and all able-bodied men who did not at once join the Secession forces were enemies. Both men managed to leave on time. A day or two earlier, a young man left Memphis under more rude circumstances, intending to return home to Indiana. Upon leaving, he thoughtlessly remarked that if the secessionists visited Fort Wayne, they would be clubbed. The shriek of "Abolitionist!" was broached, and he was summarily knocked down, beaten and taken to a barbershop, where his head was shaved. He was held overnight, and in the morning, he left for the North.[18]

Two weeks before this, a moulder and two carpenters, thought to have returned North, "were seen hanging to trees a short distance from Memphis."[19] The committee of vigilance was permeating the city with fear and loathing.

The *Louisville Journal* spelled out the transformation that the vigilance committee had rendered. Its men had given in to maliciously obsessed lunacy.

*Insane fury appears to possess their souls. They tolerate…tyranny…and… glory in upholding it. They are under the remorseless government of an irresponsible little mob, calling itself a Vigilance Committee. All their affairs are controlled by that Committee. It is for the Committee to say who may live in the city…what newspapers may be permitted…and what ones must be banned…what steamboat cargoes must be confiscated…who must be imprisoned, who whipped, who have his head shaved, who be tarred and feathered, and who hung.[20]*

By late May, it was reckoned that the committee of vigilance had driven out more than five thousand worthy and peaceable citizens whose property was virtually confiscated. This pogrom was stimulated by the February vote on secession giving the pro-Union forces in the city a majority. Whether Southern or Northern born, the slightest suspicion of being an abolitionist caused offenders to be dragooned before the committee of safety. The committee was headed by the wealthy grocer named Frazier Titus. His minions fashioned themselves the city's "first citizens." The vigilance court was constantly in session at Titus's block and processed an average of more than one hundred litigations a day. Cases included the conviction of a young Illinoisan charged with saying he would not fight his friends in Cairo. He was ordered out of Memphis on the next northbound train. Eight men, after having their heads half shaved, were banished from Memphis, while three were under death sentences when they departed.[21]

Such committees were not limited to larger cities such as Memphis. For example, Brownsville had its committee of vigilance. Until May 1861, the Right Reverend Mr. Cooper, the head of a women's seminary, was evidently a favorite personage in town. Despite his popularity, he had to leave the town on short notice because a few weeks earlier, a visiting delegation from the local committee of vigilance stopped at his dwelling and succinctly "gave him his choice…to make a secession speech, to enlist in a secession corps, or to leave the town." He did none of these things, but a week later, he and other "abolitionists" received the following preprinted and widely distributed notice:[22]

*All citizens or residents among us of Northern or foreign birth will be allowed ten days to leave our community if they so desire, but after that time no such citizens or residents shall be permitted to leave, but we shall expect all such to stand by and aid us in defending ourselves against invasion, and to all such we pledge the protection of the community, by order of the Committee of Vigilance.*

*May 24, 1861. JAS. WHITELAW, Sec'y.*[23]

After ten days, they would be forbidden to leave and would be embargoed and compelled by the armed and organized vigilance committee to serve in the secessionist cause or endure dire consequences. Since no one could reasonably expect to dispose of property in ten days in an unfriendly market, the notice served as a virtual confiscation. The Northerners and foreigners had but one realistic option, and that was to leave without "stretching hemp." One witness from Tennessee testified that "he saw on the cars quite a number of men and women fleeing from other Tennessee towns." They "must, as they value their lives, vote for the disunion ordinance and devote themselves to the disunion cause."[24]

In early June, the Memphis Vigilance Committee, so active in spying and collecting names of abolitionists, provided comic relief to its fretful efforts to carefully guard the city from abolitionists. It seemed General P.G.T. Beauregard, who "used great endeavors to keep his movements secret," arrived in Memphis. It was challenging to remain incognito in Memphis, and soon, the committee's blue jackets arrested Beauregard as a spy. "The generalissimo of the Confederate forces had to send for General Pillow to identify him, and the hero of Camargo, Mexico, soon convinced the vigilantes that they had dug their ditch on the wrong side of the rampart of Memphian defense, whereupon Beauregard was discharged with apologies."[25] Additionally, the Memphis papers were calling the attention of the vigilance committee to the high prices for provisions charged in the city. The group's purview extended beyond arresting and deporting Northerners.[26] The Beauregard incident aside, however, the committee's activities were far from humorous.

As the June 8 vote on the secession referendum approached, a veritable reign of terror developed in Tennessee. Notable was the cathartic exodus of Union sympathizers on the eve of the election. The *Louisville Journal* noted:

*It would really seem as if when innumerable Vigilance Committees are daily and nightly at work throughout Tennessee expelling Union men and their families from the State, they might venture to permit such as shall be left on the 8th of June to exercise their right of free suffrage, but no; they are afraid, that, notwithstanding the driving of thousands into exile and the turning of the whole artillery of the late Union press of the State against the Union party, secession would still be voted down unless the polls should be girt with secession bayonets.*[27]

The Memphis Vigilance Committee and others of its ilk had driven hundreds of Union men, those in opposition to secession referendum, out of the state without even the pretense of a legal trial. The committee had taken it upon itself to search the mail for objectionable literature. Such activity was not isolated to Memphis but was likewise in Middle Tennessee. According to one report:

*The Vigilance Committee of Nashville usurps similar prerogatives and uses them defiantly…every day.…The Vigilance Committees of Brownsville and other towns in Tennessee have given public notice to all men of Northern or foreign birth to leave the State.…The Nashville Union…when… questioned as to whether Union men…would be suffered to give Union votes at the polls…answered both questions…in the negative.…The Vigilance Committees of various cities and towns and counties have ordained that each ballot cast shall be an open one, whilst the disunion organs proclaim that this will show who has the audacity to vote for the old Union    distinctly implying that whoever does so will do it as his deadly peril.*[28]

As the June 8 vote on secession approached, the Memphis Committee of Vigilance distributed a lengthy and vitriolic poster titled "TRUE MEN OF THE SOUTH TO THE RESCUE." The broadside blamed Lincoln, the Black Republicans and abolitionist spies for coercing the South into leaving the Union and, in an ironic twist, claimed "the Republicans of the North are heaping insult and injury upon friends of the South in their midst, and have forced them to leave their homes."[29] This, in part, justified the committee's program to make Memphis secure, claiming the safety of the city, indeed the entire South, required "that those living in our midst, who do not wish to abandon their allegiance to Lincoln's Government, who are in favor of negro equality and the degradation of the white race, should leave this city as soon as possible. That several men from the North, who have made their homes in this city, are true to the South, there is no doubt; but there are others whom it will not do to trust." Northern men who had made their fortunes from Southern patronage would, upon the secession vote, "prove themselves traitors. Those men must be compelled to leave here. We do not counsel force for this purpose unless a refusal is given to comply with such a demand." It was urgent that the secessionist vote be approved. The lengthy tract continued menacingly with paranoid visions of enemies within, coupled with racist rape and ruin:

> *Let the proprietors of business houses, machine, carpenter, and cabinet shops, foundries, printing-offices, paint and tailor shops, hotel and boarding houses, report immediately the names of all those who they know cannot be trusted as friends to the South. It is important that this be done—the security of our property and the safety of our families demand it. Our gallant sons, who are anxious to march wherever the service of the South requires them, wish to carry with them the consoling thought that they have not left behind them the lurking enemy, who, while lingering around their homes and firesides, would incite our negroes to insurrection, and bring the worst calamities upon our wives, our mothers, and our daughters.*
>
> *"Those who are not with us are against us." Let every citizen remember that "Eternal vigilance is the price of "Liberty.""*[30]

Fiery rhetoric and threats were not enough, the committee reckoned, to ensure a secessionist victory at the polls. A more direct form of intimidation was resorted to on Election Day. Union men were marked on the day of the election, as the name of each voter was recorded (it was entered on the poll book, on the back of the ballot, with the corresponding number entered on both) so that after the vote was counted, the Union ballots could easily be discovered and the voters attended to by the committee of vigilance. This connivance was known prior to the election and successfully deterred Union men from voting at all—or compelled them to vote for secession.[31] The story was the same in the ironically named hamlet of Yankeetown, White County, Tennessee, located 250 miles to the east of Memphis. Some twenty Union men went to the polling station there and, seeing their ballots were similarly marked, refused to vote or were harassed if they did. The thoughtful Amanda McDowell of the nearby Cherry Creek community recorded in her diary:

> *Frank Coatney voted Union, said he would do it at the risk of his life, and did it, but things got so hot that he had to leave the grounds. And Jack said they marked him and were going after him last night. And another man there swore that he did not think he would ever vote again, since it was of no use, that a man could not do as he wished like honest men ought to do, that their liberties had already been voted away by the "big bugs" of the country, and for his part he did not know that he would ever vote again.*[32]

These terrorist tactics produced a secessionist victory. And no wonder—nearly a month after the pro-secession vote, it was reported that over six thousand people had "been driven from Memphis alone, by the edicts the so-called vigilance committee, or through apprehension of mob violence." The exodus was similar in the middle and western sections of Tennessee.[33]

Charles Bolton's book *Poor Whites in the Antebellum South* argues that vigilance committees were particularly concerned with "guarding against…transient poor white men, who were perceived as…most susceptible to…appeals from the Republican Party."[34] This contention is illustrated by an incident that took place soon after the secessionist victory kindled and justified more attacks by committees of vigilance, especially in West Tennessee. Three young Kentuckians, Smith, Sullivan and Myers, had been hired out as deckhands on a coal barge to Natchez, Mississippi. After their work was finished, they came back to Memphis, expecting to continue to Louisville. Yet the Memphis Vigilance Committee prohibited any boat from leaving for Louisville. The three couldn't afford the train fare and were forced to walk.

At Covington, Tennessee, the three were arrested and examined by the vigilance committee. Nothing was found against them. They were assured by the committee chairman, H.J. Molloy, that they could continue. Molloy even gave them a pass, reading:

> *Covington Jun the 2, 1861. H.J. Smith and J.B. Myers and Suleven has Past thru this Place today and Claim to be citizens of Kentucky on examination We find Nothon Rong a Bout Said Men and Willen to Let said Men Pass on Good Conduck.*

The trio traveled until rain stopped them about a mile from Ripley, Tennessee, and they took refuge under a tree. Within minutes, a force of forty mounted Tennesseans rode up and seized them as suspicious characters. They told their story and presented their pass. Nevertheless, some of the mounted men cursed them as abolitionists and loudly demanded that they be hanged from the tree they were standing under. The prisoners insisted they were not abolitionists, that they were citizens of Kentucky and Louisville, quiet, working men with no sympathy for the abolitionist cause. Things got uglier, and the gist of the denunciations coming from the equestrians was, "Louisville and the whole of Kentucky are full of damned abolitionists.… They should all be hung.…We had better be doing the work as fast as we can." The fate of three was doubtful, but that at length, Smith and Sullivan were allowed to go. Perhaps for giving a "short answer" in his interrogation,

Myers had been executed. Smith also related that, between Memphis and Covington, they came upon another victim of a committee of vigilance, a beaten man lying "with his head shaved and his ears and the end of his nose cut off." This because he wasn't born in Dixie.[35]

One incident in Memphis revolved around the confiscation of a sketch artist's luggage, and the event's graphic rendering in *Harper's Weekly Illustrated* provides a face to the "Tennessee Taliban." The journal's artist, Mr. Davis, was stopped in Memphis:

> *He was waited upon by the Vigilance Committee, who inquired, after the fashion of those bodies, who he was, where he came from, what he was doing, where he was going, and whether he didn't need any hanging. Having obtained answers to these various queries, the Committee then proceeded to inspect Mr. Davis's trunk, which they overhauled with commendable thoroughness. Finding at the bottom of the trunk a number of sketches made for us, they examined them minutely, and each member, by way of remembering Mr. Davis, pocketed two or three of the most striking. As the only revenge Mr. Davis could take on these polite highway robbers, he sketched them in the act of despoiling him.*[36]

It was reported in July that the then–recently elected justice of the Fifth Civil District Court of Memphis I.M. Dickenson told a Yankee prisoner before him of his "profound regret that it was not his power to hang him, and from his seat in court, he denounced him as a damned abolitionist who should not be allowed to live an hour. 'Had I the power…I would cut your ears off, and nail you the door of my courtroom, and probably I shall have the pleasure yet.'" Not consoling words, to be certain; they are more like those of terrorist fanatics in spirit if not substance.

This sort of terrorism was, by now, common, but punishment was not restricted to verbal abuse. The Memphis Committee of Vigilance

> *went further, and indulged every species of cruelty—shaving the head and whipping being regarded as a slight punishment by anyone who desired to remove North. Nor is this all. In more than fifty instances…men were taken before the Vigilance Committee, and no one knows what became of them. They never came from that building alive….Their acts are all secret, and there is no concern for the men charged with being tinctured with abolitionism, so that no one cares; and thus, they go on in their wholesale murdering with impunity.*[37]

One widely printed account of a conflict with the Memphis Vigilance Committee by a Unionist Tennessean told of his arrest, imprisonment and escape from the Bluff City. The committee was the most extreme example of Southern odium toward not just abolitionists and Northerners but also persons and property known or suspected of being Unionists. Moreover, in no city in Dixie "was there a larger population of Northern men who had abandoned their principles and had become…more Southern than the Southerner." They became the committee's minions, detecting and accusing fellow Northerners of being abolitionists and spies. These men were "politically and morally lost to…principles of honor…actuated… by the selfish desire to elevate themselves even to ignoble positions, if they promise power and wealth."

Not aware of a turncoat in his midst, this Unionist wrote a letter to the *New York Tribune* describing the state of affairs in Memphis in March 1861.[38] In this letter, he expressed his astonishment at the reception given Mississippi soldiers on their way to war in the Florida theater. These sentiments stimulated a visit by "a select number of the immortal 'Vigilance Committee,' who respectfully requested to examine my effects." Their manner was civil, yet their search gave him "a tickling sensation in the region of the thorax." After a complete inspection and many questions failed to find any evidence, he was "politely informed that they 'believed me to be a ——— Abolitionist,' and intended to settle my case in the morning." He was jailed that evening, convinced it was his last night on earth.

In the morning, he was ushered before the committee's court of sixty dour-faced men, not one of whom wanted anything more than to find an excuse to execute him. Even they, however, had to admit there wasn't a shred of evidence to prove him an abolitionist or a Northern man, so they decided to hold him until their associates in Washington and Baltimore could verify his opinions. He was thrown "into an underground apartment, rendered horrible by the absence of light and air, and loathsome by the presence of the accumulated filth of years; a prison quite equal to the famous 'Blackhole of Calcutta,' in its abominations." He remained there incommunicado in ninety-five-degree heat from April 25 to June 6, 1861, living on cornbread and water.

While there, he was commonly an eyewitness to some of the "harshest punishments that…aroused a vengeance blood alone can quell.…Towards *men*, these cruelties were of daily occurrence.…More than *eighty five men have had their heads shaved and their backs lacerated by the knout since the middle of last April*.…[They] are now waiting an opportunity to return and inflict summary punishment upon the people of that doomed city."

He became inured to the daily routine floggings, but nothing prepared him for the sight a Southern man "who would be base enough and fiend enough, to lay the lash upon the back of an innocent and defenceless [*sic*] *woman*." On May 19, 1861, a young, beautiful, refined and accomplished lady from Maine who had resided in Memphis for a year was whipped for "expressing too loudly her wishes for the success of our arms." She had only the day before purchased steamer tickets but was arrested that evening and incarcerated for the night.[39] At six o'clock the next morning,

> *she was brought in front of the rear door of the jail….And after three men had been whipped with the knout, and their heads shaved, she was stripped to the waist, and thirteen lashes given her with a strap, and right side of her head shaved.*[40]

He managed his escape on June 6 and hid "with an old Irish woman" before he left Memphis via train to Jackson, Tennessee. From that point, he walked to Cairo, Illinois, 120 miles through a section of country where he would be quickly hanged if he ran into a local committee of safety. After a three-day trek, he reached "the land of promise."[41]

The story of the flogging of the "refined and accomplished lady from Maine" is repeated in another Northern newspaper with a few variations. In the second version, also dated May 19, the refined lady is named Miss Giernstein. She and three male companions were abruptly spirited away from the train because of her judgmental remarks about the South. Vigilance committee thugs took them to the prison, where her three male companions were stripped naked and whipped. The thrashing was administered by a Black man with a knout some twenty-four feet in length, "which cuts the flesh in stripes an inch in width." After indignantly refusing to unfasten the upper part of her dress, the vigilance jailors "tore up her dress town to the waist. Her feet were then tied with straps." The Ohioan and the New Yorker held her arms, and the Black man "administered the stripes to her bare back." While being flogged, "the brave girl did not gratify her persecutors by a single cry or tear, but [the]…blood upon her lips, indicate[d]…she had bitten them through in suppressing…outward indications of her agony. The right side of her head was then shaved, and thus scarred and disfigured, she was permitted to resume her journey towards civilization."[42]

Like his counterpart in Nashville, Memphis mayor John Park attempted to put a damper on the activities of the vigilance committee. He issued a proclamation on August 24, 1861, that indicates the committee was impressing men into the service and otherwise committing acts of violence completely outside the boundaries of civil law. According to His Honor:

> *To the Citizens of Memphis—Applications have repeatedly been made to me, as executive officer of the city, for protection against indiscreet parties who are sent out to impress citizens into the service against their will on steamboats. Many of these men have been dragged from their beds, wives and children, but never has there been a man taken who had on a clean shirt.*[43] *I hereby notify any citizens who may wish to pass within the city of Memphis to call on me, and I will furnish the same, and will see he will be protected. One poor man being shot yesterday by one of these outlaws, as they may be called, causes me to give the above notice.*
> *August 24, 1861*
> *JOHN PARK, Mayor*[44]

One needn't be of Northern birth; he only had to travel north to run afoul of the committee of vigilance. In late August 1861, two men arrived in Nashville from New Orleans at ten o'clock Saturday morning. Their baggage was quickly transferred to the L&N Depot. One of the gentlemen bought tickets for his entire party, both men and women, and they boarded the cars anticipating no harassment. But because they had no passports, they were all taken off the passenger car. It was no simple matter to obtain them. All managed to find citizens to vouch for their identities. They left on the afternoon train and were surprised yet again that just before reaching the state line, 140 personal letters and documents were taken from their pockets to be carried back to the Nashville Vigilance Committee. Even a Confederate lieutenant returning from Richmond had 40 letters from his command to friends and family seized and taken to Nashville for scrutiny by the committee.[45]

The expulsion of Tennessee's Union citizens by vigilance committees was extended not only to regular citizens but also to national figures sitting in high positions in the national government. It was ironic and even more sensational then when the self-constituted and extralegal Nashville Vigilance Committee summarily expelled United States Supreme Court associate justice John Catron from the Tennessee capital.

Judge Catron of Nashville was one of the judges appointed to the Supreme Court of the United States by President Andrew Jackson.[46] Catron made a charge to the grand jury in St. Louis, in which he gave his views about what constituted treason. The publication of his antisecessionist views created a good deal of consternation in the Nashville Vigilance Committee. The *Nashville Gazette* observed his appearance in Nashville, noting he did not appreciate the "thousands of…brave sons he has designated as traitors, [that] he outrages the tenderest feelings of the fathers, mothers, brothers, sisters, wives and children of those gone to fight the battles of their country."[47] Yet the judge was not without friends. Stalwart secessionist V.K. Stevenson, the president of the Nashville and Chattanooga Railroad, interviewed the judge and was convinced there was nothing dangerous in his principles or intentions and that he was certain his presence in the capital would prove no danger to the newly forming Confederacy. Catron assured him he had not authorized the publication of the remarks that had caused such uproar.

Notwithstanding Stevenson's sincere endorsement of the judge, the Nashville Vigilance Committee visited him and screeched out his paranoid ultimatum: he would either be forcibly driven out of his native Nashville, home and state or publicly and robustly support secession. He was expected to give his answer at once, a demand that was softened to twenty-four hours. Catron decided to leave Nashville, leaving his sick and aged spouse behind. He boarded an L&N train and was said to have arrived in Louisville. One newspaper commented that the Nashville Committee of Vigilance "have done a deed at which the whole respectable portion of the people of the United States will raise the cry of 'shame.'"[48]

Around 1855, two young Philadelphia printers left the City of Brotherly Love for the City of Rocks and found gainful work at the Southern Methodist Publication House in Nashville and remained with the company. They earned the respect and friendship of many native Nashvillians, many of whom regretted their departure as a result of President Jefferson C. Davis's August 14, 1861 proclamation. It obliged all Northern men to leave within forty days and required them to leave their jobs to go home.[49] The two understood the meaning of the proclamation and left Nashville on the next northbound train. The night before making their exodus, the two printers made a friendly visit to James T. Bell, the city editor of the *Daily Gazette*, to say goodbye. Their conversation was private and pleasant; Bell told them he could find no fault in their leaving, that their allegiances and feelings compelled them to go. They shook hands and said amicable farewell. Unknown to the two Philadelphians, an article appeared in Bell's department of the following morning's *Gazette* under the heading "Stampede Among Printers." In vitriolic prose inspired by the vigilance committee's practices, Bell portrayed the two as a class of ingrates. Ever since Davis's proclamation they *have been seen in groups upon our street corners, evidently consulting in regard to sudden movements. They have been holding a good situation for several years past, continuing no doubt lately* [to send] *a portion of their wages to assist in subjugating the people who have fed them, acting too, probably, as spies in our midst communication such intelligence as has recently been seen in the Northern papers under the head of "Nashville Correspondence." They would have been perfectly willing to have continued at work, and given us the benefit of their* amiable *presence, had it not been for the proclamation and the "forty days" notice. Let us feel thankful that the proper means have been adopted to rid the cities of the South of such vampires.*

The two were searched, harassed, threatened and had their belongings confiscated by the Clarksville Committee of Vigilance.[50]

On September 23, 1861, the Memphis Civilian Military Committee, whose membership consisted of men of influence and wealth, were empowered by Major General Leonidas Polk to issue orders to maintain security. The military committee helped underwrite the activities of the vigilance committee. In early September 1861, by the authority vested in them by General Leonidas Polk, the committees issued orders to increase vigilance under the passport system—not to keep "Northerners" from visiting Memphis but to manage their egress; to limit or altogether terminate soldiers' furloughs, as they talked too freely about camp conditions spreading "a spirit of disquiet amongst our own people, and can easily picked up a communicated by spies"; and civilian access to military camps because they "have talked freely and publicly of misunderstandings amongst officers, of demoralization of the troops, &c., all of which you will at once see is calculated to bring the service into disrepute and perhaps cripple the efficiency of our army."[51]

But there were unintended consequences. It seems that the committee of vigilance had, in its feverish haste to rid the city and countryside of alleged abolitionist provocateurs and Northerners, shot itself in the foot. It found the city was facing an unforeseen threat it could not face alone. The harshness of the committee needed softening. Writing to Jefferson Davis, Mayor John H. Park called his attention to a phenomenon in East Tennessee, where "a large portion of our fellow citizens in East Tennessee who have for some time past been greatly disaffected to our Government have of late signified their loyalty to the South by taking the oath of allegiance." Not only that, but they volunteered for service in the Army of Tennessee after being assured their property and position would be restored to them. Some, however, remained suspicious that they would remain immune from arrest and punishment. They were informed that a large group was found in Kentucky, near the Tennessee line, that asserted intent to stay in Kentucky. If so, they would soon join federal forces. The petitioners were fearful "that they will by some means be induced to join the Federal forces, we are exceedingly anxious to make every effort to bring them to our support." Would the president give them assurances of amnesty, a policy followed in East Tennessee?[52] "We therefore desire to urge upon your Excellency the importance of giving them such assurances of protection as will effect this object?" The petition was signed by the mayor, the hierarchy of the vigilance committee and by Governor Isham Harris, who intoned "believing that it will be both right and politic to give the assurance sought to all of those misguided citizens who will in good faith return to their homes and declare their loyalty to the Government."[53] The program does not appear to have been implemented, and if it was, it had its desired effect.

In early December 1861, a curious note appeared from Sam Tate to Major General Leonidas Polk. It indicated that the committee of vigilance had lost its zeal. Tate was seriously concerned that there were "more spies in the country than I ever saw." He advised travel restrictions and the hanging of spies as a solution but warned the general: "Don't turn any more men over to the Memphis Safety Committee unless you want them turned loose."[54]

It is difficult to make more of this remark than its face value. There is no hard evidence to suggest the Memphis Vigilance Committee just faded away, and it is more probable that it continued its work with zeal, although with diminished results inasmuch it had probably rid the city of all abolitionist demons. It had apparently turned its attention to more petty matters of city government. For example, on April 15, 1862, the vigilance committee, at a regular meeting of the Memphis Board of Mayor and Aldermen, presented a resolution to reinstate a city policy officer, the cause for his dismissal not being sufficient in the opinion of the board. The case revolved around the charge that the officer had been discourteous to a lady of "impure character." The mayor reinstated the officer."[55]

As the federal armies occupied Middle and West Tennessee, the committee of public safety and vigilance "skedaddled" from Nashville, Memphis and other venues. Little was said of them, especially in the Southern press, although there was some taunting and satire in the opposing newspapers. For example, soon after the mass departure of Confederate officials and the army from Nashville, the *Louisville Journal* reported: "Nashville, if not taken, is evidently in peril. Where is her famous 'Vigilance Committee' that was so active a few months ago? Why doesn't it notify the United States army, as it did hundreds of private citizens, to leave within ten days?"[56] A satirical "review" of Reverend Dr. McFerrin's *Confederate Primer* pointed out that the most merciful men were "The Nashville Vigilance Committee, for they saved their victims the suspense of a trial."[57]

Committees of safety and vigilance were among the very first to abandon ship when the victorious Union army approached. Yet the committee of vigilance phenomenon remained where Confederate forces still occupied urban areas in Tennessee. For example, Chattanooga remained in Rebel hands until August 1863. An article cited from the *Chattanooga Rebel* in the *Nashville Patriot* in early April indicated the Chattanooga Vigilance Committee was active and proposed to hold hostages as a means of deterring the advance of the federal army. It was reported that at a meeting of the committee, it was "determined to put to death fifteen or twenty of the prominent Union men of that vicinity upon the approach of the National army." Desperate men make desperate threats, and the *Patriot* called for retribution in kind:

> *If it be found that the Vigilance Committee are really determined, in the event of the marching of our troops upon their place, let that number or twice that number of prominent rebels of Nashville or some other city be seized and sternly held as hostages for the safety of the threatened victims.*[58]

Hostages or no, the most concise comment on the terroristic nature of committees of safety and vigilance was a slogan seen on one of a plethora of banners in the grand procession commemorating the first anniversary of the fall of Memphis. It ready simply: "The reign of terror of the Safety Committee has passed away forever."[59]

# 2

# PARADES

cliché has it that "everybody loves a parade." Parades are public spectacles held to pay homage and celebrate a given cause, group or historical event. They serve the function of reinforcing social status, political norms and any of a great number of events and causes. In Tennessee in the nineteenth and early twentieth centuries, parades celebrated any number of themes, from a famous date or person in history to a civil celebration, a religious day or to recognize a myriad of interests. In a time when television, the internet and podcasts were unimaginable, parades were also just plain fun to watch. They were outlets for recognition and bestowing and reinforcing social status and esteem. Most likely, the first real manifestation of parades in Tennessee history began with the annual volunteer firemen's celebrations in Memphis and Nashville in the late antebellum era. Volunteer firemen formed a distinct social group, personified by an urban folk hero, the equivalent of David Crockett, "Mose the Bowery B'hoy."[60] The first official parade of the Memphis volunteer fire department in 1849 was a success—so much so that it was predicted by the *Memphis Daily Enquirer* "to see this beautiful display repeated."[61] In Memphis in 1855, as the annual parade of volunteers approached, the *Memphis Weekly Appeal* exhorted its readers to attend the event. It was important that the firefighters "be held in the estimation and honor that is ever grateful to the hearts of men who labor…for the public good."[62] Similar parades were held in Nashville in the antebellum era. A likeness of "Mose the Bowery B'boy," the first American urban folk hero, appeared on a float in Nashville during the 1855 parade.[63] Music, showers of flowers, more volunteer fire companies, banquets, parties, cheers, colorful uniforms, the display of decorated fire engines and speeches all helped identify the volunteers and couple pride of place with community memory. Parades continued well into the late nineteenth and early twentieth centuries, celebrating everything from military heroes, regional fairs, "baby days," military drill teams, bicycling clubs, tobacco products, automobiles and orphans to military veterans, draft horses, floral exhibitions, dolls and Tennessee's centennial in 1897.[64] They increasingly became a means of demonstrating and forging public memory with the past. Two twentieth-century events are especially worthy of attention for their historic themes. One was the reunion of the United Confederate Veterans in 1909 and the centennial celebration and parade commemorating Andrew Jackson's victory over the British at the Battle of New Orleans, held on January 15, 1915.[65]

The occasion for the notable "monster parade" in Memphis was the nineteenth reunion celebration of the United Confederate Veterans (UCV) Association, held in Memphis from June 8 to June 10, 1909. There, the veterans congregated, as did the Sons of United Veterans (SUV).[66] The commander in chief of the SUV promised to carry on the group's annual reunions "when the old veterans pass away." At their meeting, "the assemblage was conspicuous for the presence of hundreds of Confederate Dames and daughters who cheered the younger generation in their routine work of perpetuating their organization for carrying out the work of their forefathers." A distinctive feature of the SUV meeting occurred when Nathan Bedford Forrest III, the grandson of the Confederate cavalry officer, although he was but four years of age, was presented to the convention attired in the uniform of a general, which was made from the military clothes worn by his distinguished forefather. The enthusiasm was unbounded.[67] Later that afternoon, according to a press account: "From songs of war, from tap of drum, and shrill scream of fife; from martial uniforms and accouterments of battle, the scene in Memphis changed this afternoon at the Confederate reunion to dainty femininity in Paris gowns and flowers." Following the SUV meeting, an "elegant floral parade charmed both visitors and veterans as well." And no wonder, as it consisted of over one hundred stylish horse-drawn carriages adorned with the most "exquisite blossoms of the Southland, carrying the flower and beauty of Southern womanhood." It was a variegated pageant with all manner of color combinations. Each vehicle was accompanied by two or more equestrian male escorts who wore the colors of "the ladies whom they attended."

The Ladies' Hermitage Society lays a wreath at the foot of the equestrian statue of General Andrew Jackson, January 8, 1915. *Courtesy of the Tennessee State Library and Archives.*

A reenactment of the Battle of New Orleans at the centennial celebration, January 15, 1915. *Courtesy of the Tennessee State Library and Archives.*

Twenty marching bands and squads of marching veterans were interspersed in the parade. A special highlight was the display of one hundred mounted United Confederate Veteran cavalry officers. Young girls, each attired in "snowy white," were at each officer's side. Problems associated with the senectitude of some of the elder veterans were exacerbated by the heat and humidity, resulting in "a score or more prostrations—two fatal—most of the victims being the old men in gray." Nevertheless, the floral parade continued, lasting three hours. The crowd of spectators was estimated at a staggering one hundred thousand.[68]

According to the official UCV program, June 9 was taken up with UCV Association business, receptions by the United Daughters of the Confederacy and similar groups, a boat ride on the Mississippi River and a concert by the Confederate Choir at Confederate Hall.[69] The next day's events, however, were less subdued. The events of June 10 began in the morning with the "'Yip!' 'Yip!' of the famous rebel yell....One distinguished old gentleman, whose insignia told that he held a commission as Colonel, turned the yell loose in the corridors of the Gayoso Hotel, adding: 'Wake up gentlemen: wake up and put some life into this reunion!'" In the meantime, trains, which were "strung out for miles," began arriving, bringing countless visitors to Memphis to witness the parade. That morning, the reunion was held at the Bijou Theater. Speeches were made extolling the brave old soldiers of the "Lost Cause." Governor Malcom Patterson, mentioning that his father was a Confederate soldier, extended a warm welcome to the assembled veterans. His speech was followed by remarks made by the commander in chief of the Confederate Veterans, Clement A. Evans, who helped set the tone of the reunion by saying: "No! No! Our cause was not lost because it was not wrong!"[70]

The stage was decorated with the Confederate flags interwoven with United States flags. Grouped around the speakers stand were gray-clad officers of the old Confederacy, "their gold insignia on coat sleeve and collar relieving the dull gray of their uniform." Behind the senior veterans sat "the maids, matrons and sponsors in dainty white," while above them in tiers were grouped the one hundred beautiful girls, clad in gray homespun, who composed "the famous Confederate Choir." Immediately preceding Governor Malcom Patterson's speech, "the commander-in-chief of the choir...sang 'Dixie'...with a voice of wondrous charm, carrying...the silken banner of the Lost Cause....Nearly every man [on] stage stood up. Heels clicked together with military precision, and hands rose up sharply... in military salute." A cacophony of Rebel yells resounded as the last words of the Confederate anthem ("to live and die in Dixie!") were sung. The attending veterans threw their hats in the air, "hugged one another, and more than one broke into tears." The hall was a dramatic vision of waving "Stars and Bars," and the "music of the band was drowned out by the cheers."[71] After calm replaced the uproar, the meeting was adjourned. The erstwhile soldiers began assembling for the highlight of the day, their Brobdingnagian parade.[72]

After some initial delay, the parade was ready to begin. Some of the veterans had assembled as early at 5:30 a.m. A mounted squad of parade police led a forty-member marching band. More than two hundred thousand men, women and children and general followers of the surviving members of the Confederate army participated in the parade as a monstrous crowd of two hundred thousand spectators packed the sidewalks and watched from windows along the parade route, awaiting the veteran Confederate old-timers' march.[73]

It was described as the longest, biggest and greatest spectacle ever held in the city, being several miles in length. Major General John Hugh McDowell had organized the event, while commander in chief of the Confederate Veterans, General Clement A. Evans, waited for the command to kick off the procession. The regiments of veteran marchers stretched out from South Second Street to North Main Street. The command "fall in" was given, and the march began at precisely 10:00 a.m., with the veterans stepping "unflinching, unshirking and unshrinklingly [sic]," north on Second Street to Poplar Street and then to the public square and through Third, Union and Fifth Streets. As far as the eye could see, two compact lines of expectant spectators watched the approach of the leader of the parade, General Clement A. Evans, who, with "long gray locks [swept] from his uncovered head like the plumes of an eagle," was mounted on a "Kentucky bred saddler."[74] The veterans of the Army of Northern Virginia were next in line, followed by Texans and Mississippians. Third in line were Army of Tennessee veterans.

As they came into view, the "crowd on the grandstand lost control of itself and gave way to cheer after cheer."[75]

There was a break in the procession, and the crowd began to grow listless. However, soon, a "tiny tad, a boy about 3 years old, astride of a pony not much bigger than a watch dog, [came] ambling into view. A man walk[ed] at the pony's rein, using one hand to guide the animal and the other occasionally to steady the little fellow in the saddle," by now a recognized icon of the veterans' celebration.

Members of Company B. *Library of Congress.*

*It is Nathan Bedford Forrest III, the great grandson of the Wizard of the Saddle, at the head of Forrest's cavalry.* [There was no need] *to prompt the throng to cheer….If ever they gave the rebel yell, they* [gave] *it with good will.*[76]

As the equestrian General Evans approached the reviewing box, "His body was erect. His long hair waved in the vagrant wind. His eyes were bright with the memories of yesterday. His hold on his horse was firm."[77] Surrounded by his staff, he halted the parade and approached the reviewing stand, in which the son of Ulysses S. Grant, Major General Frederick D. Grant, was seated. General Grant saluted. "In a minute recognition followed, and turning his horse to one side the eminent commander of the old guard clasped the hand of Gen. Grant." This sensationally touching moment was captured for posterity by a *Commercial Appeal* newspaper photographer.

According to coverage provided by the *Memphis Commercial Appeal*:

*The meeting of the two was pathetic* [sic]. *The son of the man who was the greatest federal soldier beamed proudly. The venerated man in gray smiled back with the same look of pride. The two held hands. The vale between the blue and gray vanished. A re-united country was cemented in the clasp. Thousands of people watched. Thousands of people applauded and the parade moved on.*[78]

Having seen their commander in chief General Evans shaking hands with Grant, many of the marching veteran Rebel soldiers took the opportunity to do the same, and "it may be said in all truthfulness that Gen. Grant practically shook hands with the army of the Confederacy, or all that is left of that splendid aggregation of men who marched to victory and final defeat beneath the Stars and Bars."[79] All members of the Nathan Bedford Forrest contingent dismounted, eagerly approaching the reviewing stand to meet the son of their one-time nemesis. "Hats were thrown into the air and loud salvos of applause were sent out on every side. One old private kissed the modest general, who, with tears in his eyes, returned the salutes of the men in gray. It was sometime before order was restored and the march continued."[80] Brief conversations between a few of the veterans and General Grant were reported:

*"I fought your old daddy as hard as I could and he was a good fighter,"* said one gray veteran. *"Where did you meet him?"* asked Gen. Grant. *"I was*

*down in Shenandoah with Lee," came the reply. "I am with the Virginia troop." "I am glad I have met you. I was with my father for a while in Virginia and knew what good fighting was." Another pushed in, bent and broken. "I am proud to shake hands with General Grant's son," he said. "I tried to land him once, but I am glad to shake hands with the son of a good fighter and a good man."*[81]

Although the ranks of the Confederate veterans had thinned over the years, the enthusiasm of the spectators was palpable, as was the general feeling that this was a historic event.

Although a cool breeze blew off the Mississippi River, it failed to stifle the high temperatures, said to have been the warmest weather experienced in a number of years. But any doubts on the part of the veterans' company officers to take their men out into the heat had dissipated. "The sun beat down pitilessly upon the asphalt streets and was thrown back into the faces of the heavily clad veterans as they marched along."[82] Weaker, feebler veterans were discouraged from marching, but the martial sounds of the drum and the clatter of horses' hooves revived their spirits, and "it was with great difficulty that some of the weaker veterans were dissuaded from entering on the parade route."[83]

At times, the picture was poignant, as "men marched by without arms and rode by without legs....Others, too feeble to ride or walk were seated in vehicles and the weak voices of age enthusiastically responded to the cheering of the spectators."[84]

Nevertheless, many veterans succumbed to the extraordinary exertion, and quite a number were forced to leave the ranks of the parade before it concluded. In anticipation of such occurrences, ambulances were stationed along the line of the march to assist any vacillating marchers whose "confidence had been stronger than his powers of physical endurance." "Characteristic," noted the *Commercial Appeal*, "of the soldiers of the Confederacy these men think that there is nothing impossible for them."

Company B from Nashville came next. They kept cadence and captivated spectators all along the parade route, who greeted them with loud cheers. A number of enterprising filmmakers recorded the parade from various angles for movies to be projected later "in dizzy haste across the white screen of many moving picture shows."[85]

Aside from the veterans, women were represented as well. In Memphis, the "Southern Mothers" organization was formed in 1861 to care for wounded and sick Confederate soldiers.[86] Their role was honored with a place in the parade.

Additionally, the Daughters of the Confederacy were represented. They did not march; instead, they rode, sporting ostrich plumed hats, in elegant phaetons, befitting their social status.[87]

The Sons of Confederate Veterans, "several thousand strong," closed the parade. It was noted that they were mostly "getting along in years, nearly all of them are gray and they look like veterans themselves." There was one fatality reported from the ranks of the parading veterans.[88]

A reporter for the *Commercial Appeal* offered this romantic summation of the parade:

> *Undaunted, unappalled, undismayed, and unawed, these men went into battle against overwhelming odds and fought for four fierce years, in which they suffered every imaginable hardship. They fought to a dogged and indomitable finish, and the spirit which animated them in the bloody days was shown in the fortitude of yesterday, for, physically weak, they marched unafraid with a firm and steady tread on the hot asphalt and under a hotter sun. The faces of some were white and tired and haggard before the march was half done, but their steps never faltered and their heads were defiantly unbending.*[89]

For all intents and purposes, when the parade ended, so did the nineteenth annual reunion. Yet while the parade was over, there was still the matter of the ball that was given for the sponsors and maids. It was appropriate that the close of the greatest reunion of the United Confederate Veterans should be concluded with a social event.

The climax of the week's events came for "not only the younger generation but the veterans as well…at the ball given for the sponsors and maids.…It was fitting that the close of the greatest reunion of the United Confederate Veterans should be closed with mirth and music." The ball was held at the large auditorium on Madison Avenue, with room for ten thousand attendees. The floor accommodated fully seven thousand dancers, while the venue was decorated with Confederate flags presenting "a vivid scene of color.… Thousands of Confederate uniforms were in evidence and on tier after tier were banked solidly the long rows of ladies and their escorts who came to view the ball."[90] The crowd became so numerous that the city building commissioner ordered the doors be closed to maintain safety. The ball was "opened by the famous Southern Cross Drill and 1,000 couples participated in the dance, despite the suffocating heat."[91] Apparently, as the evening wore on, a pair of mounted veteran cavalry officers managed to enter the dance floor, and "in some manner unexplainable, their horses collided in such a way that both gentlemen were thrown to the ground." Neither was critically injured, although one of them was "unable to walk home."[92] The nineteenth annual reunion of the United Confederate Veterans concluded and was itself a historical event.[93]

The celebration of the centennial of the Battle of New Orleans, the famous victory of the United States over the British on January 8, 1815, was attended by a large audience of spectators. It was to be a grand celebration of "Jackson Day," an annual event that had been observed in less dramatic fashion each January 8, generally with the active involvement of the exclusive guardians of the seventh president's reputation and residence, the Ladies' Hermitage Association. The event featured a parade, a sham battle, a wreath laying, speeches and a banquet but was not as enormous a spectacle as the Confederate veterans' episode in Memphis six years earlier.

The "mammoth parade" was led by principal representatives of every branch of Nashville's bourgeois business, society and civic life. The parade, seen by thousands, was formed at Ninth Avenue and Broadway and proceeded east to Second Avenue and then to the public square. From that point, it was to progress to Fourth Avenue and Deaderick Street and then from there to Fourth Avenue and Church Street, continuing until it reached Eighth Avenue, where it was "systematically dispersed." The crowd was then divided and returned to the boulevard and Church Street to limit any confusion. Features of the parade included a long line of automobiles carrying members of the Confederate women's societies of the city, while members of the Commercial Club and the Ladies' Hermitage Association and members of the Andrew Jackson Memorial Association were conspicuous. Hundreds of citizens in public life throughout the state participated in the event, which was organized "to perpetuate the name and fame of 'Old Hickory.'" It was noted that the event likewise celebrated a century of peace between Great Britain and the United States and brought attention to the Jackson Memorial Association Fund.

Led by marching bands, Nashville's Fire and Police Departments joined in the "mammoth procession" as well. The city police department was represented by a twenty-four-member mounted contingent, and the "fire laddies" paraded on foot. City officials took the lead in the procession; they were followed by companies of uniformed Confederate cavalry and infantry veterans, companies of the Tennessee National Guard and representatives from the Young Men's Christian Association, the Commercial Club, the Nashville Business Men's Association, the Builder's Exchange, the humane association, the Tennessee Children's Home Society and the Women's Equality League. Other civic organizations participated in the parade as well. A special squad of police was on hand to facilitate traffic and handle the expected throng. A special brigade of coonskin cap–wearing volunteer horsemen had been recruited to represent the soldiers of Tennessee and Kentucky who took so prominent a part in the Battle of New Orleans. The brigade was to be augmented by other similarly attired volunteer horsemen led by the Davidson County sheriff.

A major feature of the event was a "sham battle," a reenactment of Jackson's victory at New Orleans one hundred years earlier. The replica battle scene exceeded all other attractions of the centennial celebration. Companies H and K of the Tennessee National Guard took on the role of the British. Confederate veteran Troop A and Company B were designated to play the part of American forces led by "Old Hickory" Andrew Jackson. The Tennessee Guard troops were dressed in "light marching order" brown, not in replicas of the colorful red garb of British soldiers of a century earlier. The battle itself was choreographed and directed by national guard officers. The Confederate veterans were clad in their gray uniforms.[94] After a few remarks by politicians and local business leaders, the much-anticipated sham battle began. According to a newspaper account:

> *One feature of the Battle of New Orleans was brought out when many cotton bales were thrown up as a breast works on the west side of the wide Capitol boulevard and behind this the Confederates impersonated the soldiers of Old Hickory.…The steady and incessant clatter of the rapid firing guns of the modernly equipped militiamen and the boom of the old model rifles of the Confederates made day hideous for a few minutes before the militia began to retreat even as the British did under Packenham.*
>
> *The militia covered their movements by hiding behind a wall until at a signal of their officers they dashed from undercover and made for the breastworks. The fire from the old rifles was too much and they fell back in bad order and the day was won for the soldiers of the phantom leader, Old Hickory Jackson. As the rattle of guns became subdued a dozen white doves, signals of peace, were released by little girls for the Ladies' Hermitage Association.*[95]

After the battle had been won and the cheers had dwindled, speeches were given extoling the heroic bravery and self-sacrificing, heroic and patriotic qualities of Andrew Jackson. The speakers included governor-elect

Thomas Rye and *Nashville Banner* newspaper editor John Stallman. Following their tribute, there was a wreath laying ceremony at the equestrian statue of General Jackson on the Tennessee Capitol grounds, "the most beautiful and impressive ceremonies of the great event."

It fell to the Ladies' Hermitage Association, the civic cult of Andrew Jackson, to solemnly gather and place wreaths at the base of the red-white-and-blue-bunting-draped base of the sculpture in honor of the object of their devotion. The principal speaker, the first regent of the Ladies Hermitage Association, made remarks:

> *It is due that we should revere and commemorate as we have on this occasion, their deeds of valor and sacrifice and pay just tribute to Tennessee's greatest soldier and statesman, the American patriot without a peer, Andrew Jackson.*

After her remarks, another "fifteen white doves were liberated by little girls," and after "flying over the battlefield, soldiery and thousands of citizens the homer [*sic*] pigeons flew in different directions."[96] There followed a ceremony of laying wreaths "by several prominent members of the association and leaders in Nashville society and club life" at the equestrian statue of Andrew Jackson. The first regent of the Ladies Hermitage Association said, "I place this in tribute to the man who made us all free American born citizens today."[97]

Another wreath was placed at the base of the statue by Mrs. Bettie M. Donelson, who remarked, "One hundred years ago at the Battle of New Orleans—Sir Edward Packenham's army's watchword was 'beauty and booty.' As one of the organizers of the Ladies' Hermitage Association, I honor Andrew Jackson as the protector of 'beauty and booty' and take pleasure in placing this this simple wreath on his monument."

A total of fifteen wreaths were placed at the base of the monument. Later that night, a grand Jackson Day ball was held for an audience of leading citizens and members of Nashville's fashionable society. Said to be "the biggest event on the program," it was held appropriately enough at the Hermitage Hotel. "This affair is being keenly anticipated, especially by the younger set, and it should prove one of the most pleasing features." It was not open to the public; instead, it was restricted to a circumscribed list of elite invited attendees.

"The Ladies' Hermitage Association made its celebration of one of one of the most important epochs of our history…a brilliant success." The decorations in the ballroom and the logia of the hotel were of a "patriotic nature.…Hundreds of American flags and interesting relics of former wars in the shape of rifles and swords occupied places of honor." The speakers' platform was decorated with shields of the states of Louisiana and Tennessee, while cotton balls were the most common decoration in the ballroom, "and great ropes of Jackson vine studded with [cotton] balls six inches in [diameter] were suspended across the room forming an artistic canopy." Dinner was served at midnight.[98]

These two events were about more than parades and public entertainment, although they certainly did fulfill that purpose. They served as demonstrations to solidify the social status and political power of Civil War veterans and those who venerated Andrew Jackson. It is not going too far to suggest, as Dr. Tom Kannon has perspicaciously submitted, that such parades and celebrations are about more than mere demonstrations of public memory but are indeed a means of "some interests exerting more power than others," employing the past as a means of solidifying social and political influence in the present.[99] In both instances, however, public demonstrations, such as the parade of the United Confederate Veterans in Memphis in 1909 and the Centennial of the Battle of New Orleans, have waned to near obscurity. Indeed, indicative of the loss of public reminiscence, there was no giant procession to celebrate the bicentennial of the Battle of New Orleans in 2015, and unsurprisingly, as the mortality of Confederate veterans necessarily led to the absolute decline of their numbers, celebrations of the history these two events has largely been diminished in public memory.

# 3

# TENNESSEE MILITARY DRILL TEAMS

## *Circa 1874–1887*

etween 1874 and 1887 and to the end of the nineteenth century, military drill teams were a phenomenon of urban life in Tennessee and indeed the entire nation. They were part of private and independent militia companies incorporated according to Tennessee state law and not a part of any organized state guard or militia until 1887.[100] At that time, being in uniform meant that one identified with the company of which you were a member as well as the urban area in which the company was located. There are but few if any real examples of these companies being utilized in any real martial manner. These companies sported teams that performed military drills in competitions often called "encampments." As far as can be determined, the first such organizations were established in 1874. One in Memphis was named the "Chickasaw Guards," chartered on June 30; another, the Nashville Porter Rifles, was organized on May 11, 1874.[101] In addition to these companies, sometime before August 1875, the O'Conner Zouaves organized in Knoxville, while in the same year, a plethora of such military companies were formed across the state.[102] By September 1875, twenty-seven independent, private militia companies formed the so-called Centennial Brigade.

In East Tennessee, there were the O'Conner Zouaves; Dickinson Light Guards; Light Guard and James Guards (Chattanooga); Johnson Guards (Greenville); Tennessee Volunteers (Union Depot); and the Jefferson Guards (Strawberry Plains).

In Middle Tennessee, there were the Grays and Blues, the Jackson Guards, the Porter Rifles and the Bate Reserves (Nashville); the McEwen Rifles (Franklin); the Spence Guards (Murfreesboro); the Trousdale Guards (Gallatin); and the Brown Guards (Pulaski).

From West Tennessee came the Memphis Grays, the Irish Volunteers and the Stonewall Grays (Memphis); the Stonewell Guards (Dresden); the Hambey Guards (Pickett Ville); the Henderson Light Guard (Bolivar); the Chickasaw Guards and Centennial Guards (Brownsville); the Tennessee Rifles (Dyersburg); the Bellville Guards (Bell's Depot); the Centennial Guard (Alamo); the Porter Guards (Humboldt); and the Trenton Guards (Trenton).[103]

The approaching national centennial seems to have been the spark that led to the formation of these private military drill teams. Their status was semiofficial; while they were not part of any militia or state guard, they were considered as independent and private units of a state militia that had no de jure sanction. Their drill competitions helped define the status of Tennessee cities—typically, after the national centennial, Nashville and Memphis. They provided entertainment and identifiers for their cities and were actually more like baseball teams in their following, but they predated the coming of professional baseball by ten years.[104]

Teams would meet and visit upon invitation from other cities' teams. For example, on August 30, 1875, there "was a gala time long to be remembered in Knoxville," when the "citizen soldiery" were inspected by the military staff of the governor in "the presence of thousands of people." The O'Conner Zouaves and the Dickinson Light Guards made what was called "a very handsome appearance." A stand of colors was presented to the visiting Light Guards by the Zouaves as "at least ten thousand spectators" watched the spectacle. The main feature of the "holiday was the grand banquet given by Major O'Conner at the opera house.…It was a most elegant entertainment—superior beyond comparison to anything of the kind ever known in East Tennessee." The opera house was decorated with flags and evergreens, with eight tables "bending with all the vians [sic] that money could purchase and skill prepare." Four hundred guests sat down at the banquet, which ended at midnight.

*Distinguished gentlemen from all parts of the state were present. A most pleasurable evening was spent. When the toast, "Major Thomas, O'Conner," was announced, the enthusiasm was intense, and the applause lasted full five minutes. The entire four hundred guests rising to their feet, and with clapping of hands of waving of handkerchiefs, testifying their approbation of our people and great-hearted townsman, Major O'Conner.*

Major O'Conner, a local railroad and banking tycoon, gave the banquet "to the citizen soldiery" of Knoxville and many prominent citizens throughout the state. There was no drill competition, yet the nature of the early paramilitary units seems clear enough—terms such as *citizen soldiery*, *prominent citizens, banquet, four hundred citizens* and *ten thousand spectators* all denote the honor and social recognition one would accrue from being a member of an independent militia or paramilitary company.[105] There was, however, not one instance in which any of these drill companies was actually used in a military circumstance, unless drill competition and parading in dress uniforms qualified as martial activities. It was said of the Memphis Chickasaw Guards that the "social distinction of the members…made this command one of the most notable in the south."[106] Thus, the social importance of such organizations eclipsed any martial importance that may have been attributed to them.

Competitions began, it appears, in May 1875, as the nation entered its centennial, when the Porter Rifles bested the Chickasaw Guards in a drill competition. In October, the Chickasaw Guards (also known as the "Chicks") turned the tables and won a rematch competition. The Chicks again beat the Memphis Grays. The state centennial competition held in Nashville was attended by contingents from many Tennessee companies, but it was clearly a contest between the Nashville Porter Rifles and the Memphis Chickasaw Guards. Betters had the Chicks as the odds-on favorite. "They went to their arms with the air of old soldiers, receiving the applause of the assemblage in anticipation of a first-class display." Their uniforms consisted of regulation blue cloth, trimmed in red, a white band forming an X on the chest, and a blue cap with a red pompon. The only flaw in their presentation was that the company did not show "the promptness and alacrity of the [Porter] Rifles in execution." As the judges retired to make their decision, the Porter Rifles entertained the "spectators with an exhibition of their skirmish drill." In the end, the Porter Rifles unanimously won the contest, the announcement being met with extended applause. The winners' cup was described as being "of elegant design, gold lined, and supported by a spiral center piece and two guns on each side crossed."[107] The Harding Artillery of Nashville announced its new uniforms in 1884, indicating the company was more interested in show than actually fighting:

*They will be made of elegant grey cloth. The captain will wear a frock coat with red standing collar, gold lace on the sleeves, and pants with red stripe one and a quarter inches wide. The buttons will bear the coat of arms of the State. The dress of the other officers and privates will be the same with the modification marking rank. The Sergeants in place of gilt cuffs will have solid red ones. The cap of the captain also will be red with three rows of gold lace, while those of the privates will be grey with red bands or chords.*

*The company will make a very handsome appearance in the first drill in which they enter, both on account of its personnel and uniform.*[108]

The Chicks went on to win first place in a national drill competition held in Saint Louis on May 22, 1878, winning over the Chicago company, thought to be the finest drill company in the nation. In October, they defeated the Governor's Guards in Nashville's competition, winning over Nashville's Porter Guards. Memphis had a "crack team." In 1880, the Memphis team, the Invincible Chicks, carried off the second prize in a national contest in Saint Louis and retained their first place standing in Tennessee.[109] The Chicks won eight out of twelve competitions. These regional and national completions were marked by the ebb and flow of various teams claiming first prize in Columbus Ohio, New Orleans, Louisiana.[110] The uniforms of the Chicks consisted of a "blue coat and trousers, trimmed in red, white helmet with plumes and tops, and white belts and cross belts."[111] There were no hard feelings, only expressions of cordiality and honor. An editorial in the *Nashville Daily American* claimed the Porter Rifles were cultivating the proper spirit among the citizen soldiery of the Chickasaws, although the team had been defeated in 1876.

*We can truly say that we were captured early in the action by the manly breasts of the generous hearted men whom we had formerly looked upon as rivals, and succumbed to their kindness before the clash of arms began.*[112]

Yet this camaraderie was to change to acrimony after the 1877 regional completion in Huntsville, Alabama, where the Porter Rifles defeated the Chickasaw Guards for the Tennessee state championship. The medal, according to the Chickasaw Guards, should have been divided in half, inasmuch as the Guards were the state champions. A disagreement in "tactics" led the Chickasaw Guards to default and not compete with the Porter Rifles, who therefore won the competition.

The Chicks proposed to split the medal, inasmuch as they did drill in a separate but equal manner, and sent a check to the Porter Rifles for $37.50, half the cost of the medal. The Porter Rifles disagreed and refused. The Porter Rifles won fairly and squarely and invited the Chicks to another competition in 1879.

"The action taken by the Chickasaw Guards is characteristic of their proceedings at Huntsville, where they utterly failed to come up to the scratch. Now they desire to claim honors, not won in drill. To make up for this lack of merit, they 'resolve' that they are the champions of the State and attempt to make their unjust claims tenable by an attempt to hoodwinking the Porter Rifles into the surrender of the medal." The Porter Rifles kept their medal.[113] The Huntsville competition event included a banquet, "where the tables fairly groaned under the supply of edibles…by the caterer of the Chattanooga Hotel."[114]

> *The table was in the shape of an X, and five smaller tables were in various parts of the room. The flowers that were used in such profusion to ornament every part were…in abundance. The large pyramids here and there, were very handsome. A larger room adjoining had in reserve some five hundreds or thousand cakes, while long rows of roast pig, ham, etc., etc., attest to the inexhaustibility of the supply. Forty gallons of ice cream were consumed.[115]*

There were likewise separate Black companies. The Langston Rifles, the Rock City Guards, the Carson Guards and Winter's Guard hailed from Nashville, while the McClellan Guards, the Colored Zouaves and the Tennessee Rifles organized in Memphis. The two Black teams provided a great deal of help during the yellow fever epidemic in the Bluff City, especially the McClellan Guard, which patrolled the streets and protected businesses of the city.[116]

Gallatin had the Trousdale Guards; Chattanooga was the home of the Light Infantry. Murfreesboro was the home of the Sparks Rifles. The Maury Rifles were from Columbia. And from Clarksville hailed the Scipio Guards.[117] These organizations competed among themselves in a manner similar to that of the white companies and did so essentially for the same reasons. At the Huntsville, Alabama competition of 1883, it was "a grand day for our colored citizens who were in town in full force." A special excursion train from Memphis, comprising six coaches, came to Huntsville for the competitive drill. The Black contest was between the McClellan Guards

THE ATLANTA ARTILLERY.

*Top*: The Atlanta Artillery competing in a sham battle in Nashville. *Courtesy of the Tennessee State Library and Archives.*

*Bottom*: Preparing troops for a sham battle in Nashville. *Courtesy of the Tennessee State Library and Archives.*

and the Zouaves, both from Memphis. After parading in the streets in the morning, they took their places at the fairgrounds. The drill was witnessed by about 2,500 people.[118]

An interstate competition took place in Nashville between the Sumner Guards of Saint Louis and the Langston Rifles at Nashville's baseball parks on August 19, 1886. "It was quite an event in colored circles, and the amphitheater was packed." The Langston Rifles took the prize as they were "vociferously cheered by the grand stand, which was filled with the elite of colored society.…There was continued applause for the home company." A sham battle also took place, pitting the Langston Rifles, Sumner Hawkins' Rifles and the Douglas Guards against one another, attracting wide attention and praise.[119] At a local Nashville competition in June 1888, the Langston Rifles paraded to West Side Park in the morning, headed by the Immaculate Band. Their line of march went from the front of the Knights Templar lodge down Spruce Street to Line Street, and then from Line Street to Summer Street, Summer Street to Cedar Street, Cedar Street to the public square, around the square to College Street, College Street to Union Street, Union Street to Cherry Street, Cherry Street to Church Street, Church Street to Spruce Street and, finally, Spruce Street to Broad Street to West Park Street. The Langston Rifles were beaten by the Rock City Guards after a thirty-five minute drill.[120] Together with one hundred members of the local branch of the Grand Army of the Republic, both the Langston Rifles and Rock City Guards participated in celebrations commemorating the Emancipation Proclamation in what a newspaper called a "Monster Procession of the Colored People of Tennessee."[121]

In 1890, one incident involving the Langston Rifles indicates both the pride Black men took in their drill teams as well as the racial tensions that were de rigueur for Jim Crow legislation. The company, while practicing its drill in the Knowles and Church Streets environs, was passed by an electric trolley car. Witnesses stated:

> *The motor man endeavored to stop his car, but being on a rather steep grade, it continued to slide until it cut into the procession. These brave soldiers, marching four deep, presented bayonets at the breast of the motor man and acted as if they intended to spit him then and there. Upon this two police officers, in the car, came forward to protect the motor man.*
>
> *While this was going on in the rear, Thomas Prendergast, Jr., attempted to cross the street about twenty feet ahead of the procession, when the big, burly drum major seized his horse by the bit and threw him back on his haunches. The drum major, in the excitement, and in his strutting admiration of his own imposing form, had gotten far ahead of his company....He threw Mr. Prendergast's buggy back on the track and the electric car ran into his buggy. Upon this, Pendergrass [sic], who is a one-legged man and goes on crutches, hit the drum major over the head with his crutch.*
>
> *The negroes with their bayonets presented, came surging around the buggy, and the father of Prendergast hit one of them with a stone. White people and negroes from all directions came running up until quite a crowd was collected. The policemen exercised all their power in dispersing the crowd and getting the troops to move on. No arrests were made.*[122]

There were reports of similar occurrences in the two days preceding this near riot. It was not surprising that the white press condemned the Langston Rifles and called for the company's disbandment.[123] Some of the parties involved, including all members of the drill team, were arrested and were to be tried on July 7. The United Electric Railway's president petitioned Governor Robert L. Taylor, demanding the company be disbanded, claiming the Black troops were entirely at fault.[124] The officers of the Langston Rifles called upon the governor and denied all the charges made against them, asserting the streetcar broke into their ranks and nearly ran over them. An investigation was to follow.[125] What the governor decided is not known, nor is it known what happened to the parties reportedly arrested for trial. But it is known that in mid-January 1898, one hundred men of Company G of the Langston Rifles, bearing the flag Langston had presented to the company in 1885, were among the audience at the funeral service at the Howard Congregational Church held in honor of the deceased John Mercer Langston, the company's namesake, so it is most likely the company was not disbanded.[126]

Nashville was the scene for national competitions. A flyer for the 1881 competition indicates the scale and importance of the event, at least as an identifier for the city of Nashville.

An oration given to the Porter Rifles by the company's ex-chaplain in 1882 indicates the reasons a young man would want to become a citizen soldier in a private military company:

*The eyes of the world have always been cast on the soldier. Men love the measured* tramp, tramp, tramp *as the boys go marching on in long lines and bright clothing. The swords, spears, helmets, bayonets that catch the sunlight and dazzle with their reflections a thousand eyes, charm the heard to admiration and move the lips and hand to applause.…There was a time when the soldier was more dress and armor not man, now he is equipped with less, but farther reaching and more effective weapons, and less dress, and we ask amid the changing customs and clothes of soldiers, what is a soldier?*

*A soldier is not merely 125 or 150 pounds of flesh and bone, dressed in his blue pants and a blue coat with 20 brass buttons, heavy musket, and shining bayonets, but he is the representation of right or wrong. He is simply a citizen in another dress and amid other surroundings, and who has taken the bayonet instead of the ballot. Like his flag he is the embodiment of that which is most sacred and precious to his country. Not the colors, but what they represent, makes them valuable. The soldier has a prominent place in history. Every age and land has its military, its uniforms and its tactics. We cannot tell and do not know who the first soldier was, but Abraham was the first and highest officer in the first war.…From the time of the use of blunt and sharp stones, hurled by a bow or sling, from the war club and battle-ax up to the thundering cannon, clicking revolver, crashing muskets, flashing bayonets and clanking of sabers, the soldier has played an important part. The call of the bugle has rung out upon the air everywhere. The rattle of the drum has become universal. Signal fires have gleamed out upon almost every hillside and loomed up in the history of every war and country.…*

*A true soldier is a lofty type of true man. He is faithful—always at his post; dutiful-yielding all proper obedient; respectful—saluting and honoring his superiors. He is kind; he helps his sick and tired comrades carry his knapsack or gun, he prays with the wounded and turns for the moment into mother, pastor and beloved one, as he wipes the death sweat, and drop by drop it crowds through the pores and writes for the dying the last letter of the battlefield, in the hospital, and after death turns into minister, congregation and undertaker, during war times, and plants the first flower in time of peace on the graves of his defeated comrades. He is generous with his companions, sharing the last cracker and the last cup of fresh water from the canteen, and in defense of one, risks his own life. He loves his God and country.*[127]

Military drill teams also served in public services, such as those honoring the Confederate dead. In Memphis in late May 1877, the Chickasaw Guard and the Irish Volunteers of State Guard were "in full uniform" while in attendance at a wreath laying ceremony honoring Confederate dead in Memphis. "A magnificent wreath of choice flowers made by a number of Southern ladies was presented by Gen. Forrest and adorned the speakers' stand." Among the speakers was General Gideon Pillow, ex–Confederate governor Isham G. Harris and "a large number of regimental commanders."[128] The popularity of the drill competitions can be judged by events that took place in Nashville on June 18, 1877. The ascent of the gas balloon called the *Buffalo* was "for the time overshadowed by the… excitement regarding the competitive drill."[129] The interstate drill held in Nashville in 1888 attracted much attention, and a parade through the city was watched approvingly by a crowd of fifteen thousand if a newspaper account can be relied on.[130]

The March 1887 sham battles were par for the course and may have been the precursors for contemporary Civil War battle reenactments and similar to *Buffalo Bill's Wild West Show*. Teams were chosen for either defensive or offensive roles, and after blank ammunition was handed out, the soldiers went through their drills to the applause and intense interest of spectators. The sham battle, the major event of the encampment held in Nashville at the 1888 statewide competitions, was described in a newspaper account:

*The event of the day [took place when] Gen. W.H. Jackson, the noted "Red Fox" of the Confederacy, and Gen. J.B. Palmer, the sacred veteran of the Lost Cause, were to led the troops of the encampment in a sham battle. It was the desire to witness this novel spectacle that drew the vast assemblage to the Park, and excitement ran high as the time approached for its presentation. A 5 o'clock the troops began to march to their positions, Gen. Jackson's forces were on the southern boundary of the field, next to the camp, and those of Gen. Palmer on the northern limit. As the artillery rattled past the grandstand, closely followed by the infantry they were loudly cheered. The opposing armies were composed as follows. Gen. W.H. Jackson, in command; One detachment from the Rockville Artillery, Indianapolis Light Artillery, Harding Light Artillery, Washington Light Artillery, Burns and Battery E, First Ohio, the Atlanta Rifles, Louisville Light Infantry, Latham Light Guards, Merchants' Zouaves and Witt Rifles.*

*Gen. J.B. Palmer, in command: One detachment from the Atlanta Artillery, Louisiana Field Artillery, Dallas Light Artillery, Louisville Light Artillery, Baxter Artillery, Southern Cadets, Company H, Dakota Hermitage Guards, Rock City Guards, Linck Zouaves.*

*When Gen. Jackson, in full uniform and riding a thoroughbred dark bay, emerged from the camp and appeared among his men some of the "boys" or more properly, veterans who had followed him a quarter of a century ago when battle was no mimic scene, saluted their old chieftain and with the Rebel yell, and as he advanced to view the line of battle of the enemy the amphitheater greeted him with loud applause.*

*Now came Gen. Palmer, astride a mettlesome grey, his staff about him, looking scarcely older than on that memorable day when his blood stained the field of Murfreesboro. To hearty applause he galloped past the grand stand, and soon his figure became blurred among the troops far to the north. A brief pause and the battle opened. Cannon belched fire from the border of the camp and smoke had scarcely enveloped the form of Gen Jackson, who stood near his battalion, before responding thunder came from the enemy. The sublimity of the artillery duel, war's most intense emblem of carnage, stirred the pulse and warmed the blood. Puffs of smoke curling above the foliage of the trees, away across the field, told of sharpshooter sent out by [the] "Red Fox," and their rapid echoes showed that musketry supplemented the thunder to the full measure of war's music. Skirmish line had been withdrawn and each army slowly came forward in regular line of battle. Suddenly a staff officer is seen to leave the side of Jackson and dash up to captain of the Merchant Zouaves. A moment and the Memphians' wheel and deploy to the rear of the timers' stand. "Red Fox" has planned an ambush; he must silence the Galting [sic] which is creeping upon his left. As the cannonade reaches its climax, and the column of Palmer moves forward with exultant step the ambush is sprung. With the Zouave battle cry Defray spring to the front of his gallant command and waving his sword high in [the] air dashes toward the ominous Gatling. It is hastily withdrawn, but too late. Penetrating the left wing of the enemy the Merchants capture the [Gatling gun], and with it Palmer's Chief of artillery, and both are borne in triumph to the Jackson camp, the cheers of the amphitheater mingling with the music of cannon and musketry. The fire is getting hot now, and as the Louisiana Infantry charges to the right Gen. Jackson orders a retreat. This is affected slowly and in order, the troops firing as they retire. Palmer's artillery now redoubles its energy and is answered fast by Jackson's but the day was lost, and, steadily advancing, Palmer comes on to victory, Jackson's form is seen towering in the rear guard of his troops, but the enemy comes with unwavering front. A minute and the end is at hand. With a final charge Palmer's men are upon the camp of Jackson, their standards are captured and surrender follows.*[131]

Competitions were based on a group's performance of military drill regulations. These included, for infantry, maneuvers from either the Hardee or Upton's Manuals for the best drilled company and individual. Their performance was judged on accuracy and precision, whether in intra- or interstate competition. The drills for 1888's competition included the categories for interstate, state infantry, artillery, Gatling gun and Zouaves. In the individual drill, contestants were put through the manual of arms, followed by squad drill and a skirmish drill. The judges' general comments were stern and indicated that the teams were more for social distinction and show than military bearing and preparedness.

*That as a rule the pieces were rusty and dirty and the accoutrements uncared for. This is a serious neglect and no company which aspires to any distinction should be found thus careless.…The soldierly bearing of the companies is far from a proper standard and exhibited a great want of instruction in the school of the soldier without arms. Squad drill is the foundation of the company drill and every organization should devote time to it....The companies lacked the firmness and decision which practice in the elementary principles or the tactics bring about.*

*In several instances it was noticed that in marching in quick time the knees were not straightened, the gait between the springy and uncertain. In marching in line there was apparent an ever-present disposition of the files to depend on their neighbors, as in the wheeling the elbows were held out, seeming as if to hang on. The general touch of elbows should be practiced. The annual of arms was fairly well executed, save by one or two companies, where the motions were jerky and slightingly executed. In the loadings firings, the fix and unfix bayonets, there was observed an unauthorized cadence or clock-like regularity.*[132]

In the 1888 drill in the interstate infantry competition, the Louisville Light Infantry took first place; in the state competition, the Witt Rifles claimed first honors, the Indianapolis Artillery took first honors and the Linck Zouaves from Memphis took first place; and Private Jesse C. McComb of the Louisville Light Infantry won the prize for best individual drill.[133]

All the independent military companies were merged into the Tennessee National Guard in 1887.[134] It was reported in 1888 that the Chickasaw Guards were actively engaged in merging with the state guard, while the Porter Rifles had "almost disbanded. It will bring sincere regret to all to see that grand old company that won so many victories on hotly-contested fields go to pieces now, just when Tennessee for the first time has reached out her helping hand. It is hoped that the Porters will reorganize and take part in the May drill to be held in [Nashville]." The Hickory Guards were to reorganize and take the place of the Porter Rifles as the crack company of the Union.[135]

These drill competitions continued until the early twentieth century, when, gradually, regular army units of the national guard took the place of the private companies. In 1887, the Tennessee State National Guard was established.[136] A federal law authorized the states to provide "arms, ordinance stores, quartermaster stores, and camp equipage for issue to the militia" of the states. Accordingly, the state distributed among the military companies organized under the state militia's central office. The materials were distributed to the First (Middle), Second (West Tennessee) and Third (East Tennessee) Militia Regiments, which incorporated the existing military drill teams organizations, including Black companies, into the Tennessee State National Guard.[137] From this point onward, the drill competitions decreased in importance and became private clubs with individual charters, and they continued, with increasingly less attention, in competitions between various national guard units. The new competitions would eventually include such exercises as the usual close order company drill, individual drill, modern artillery, machine gun drills, tent drills, obstacle courses and a plethora of other martial activities, according to the U.S. Army's new manual of arms, or the Butts' Manual. The days of fancy parade dress uniforms with colored stripes, white belts and plume crested helmets were increasingly a thing of the past, and while the new competitions still drew attention, their occurrence dwindled until the United States' entry into the First World War in 1917.[138] Afterward, they ceased to exist in the world made safe for democracy. The competitions of the nineteenth century were more for show, with fancy uniforms, and were a means for social approbation and urban identification rather than any real military purpose.[139] The professionalization of the armed forces marked the decline of the private and independent military companies in Tennessee and indeed in the nation.[140]

# 4

# BICYCLING IN NASHVILLE ENVIRONS

## *1880s–1890s*

Bicycling in the 1880s and 1890s was essentially a gender-based, middle-class phenomenon tied closely to the growth of income and increase in leisure time. The activity ultimately crossed gender lines, both in an amature and professional capacity, and it became a social outlet and even a force for the improvement of health and good road development. Local cycling clubs were formed, recreational area races were run and interest in professional races was noted.

Bicycling symbolized the growth of leisure time and the middle class, along with increased mobility and the American focus on forming associations. The kinds of bicycles utilized were, at first, the "ordinary," which are most commonly thought of as a "high wheel," and the successor to it, the "safety," or what is today generally thought of as the standard bicycle with two identically sized wheels. The ordinary bicycle sported a high wheel with a diameter running from forty-eight to sixty inches. While ordinary bicycles were noted in Nashville in the early 1880s, it wasn't until June 1883 that the Nashville Bicycle Club was founded with nineteen members. The group's bike preference and uniform indicate that bicycling was an upper-class masculine pastime.[141]

"The members seem to favor the [ordinary] Columbia wheels that make having fourteen representatives, the Harvard three, and the American Star two.…Their colors are blue and gold. The regulation uniform consists of dark navy blue cloth, knee pants, blue flannel shirt and dark blue stockings;

bicycle cap, with peak to match, and a dark blue necktie."[142] The high-wheel bike was, because of its construction, impossible for Victorian-era women to ride, given the modesty of the times and the length of skirts, but posed no problem in that regard for men. Bicycling was, therefore, at first an essentially male activity until the introduction of the safety bike, essentially what we think of today as a bicycle. Bikes, whether of the high wheel or safety design, were typically called the "wheel" by American enthusiasts.[143] Bicycling was an excellent means of promoting health and was said to be the "best of all forms

Bicycling. *Courtesy of the Tennessee State Library and Archives.*

of health-giving exercise."[144] The first part of cycling was the confidence that one needed not to crash. Experience was the other, more essential factor. In 1889, the beginning of the "cycling season" had seen only one or two safety wheels among the estimated three hundred or more ordinary bikes. "Such was the prejudice against [safety bikes] that it was some time before others were introduced." The bias melted away as the superiority of the safety over the ordinary became manifest, and by August 1889, nearly half the bicycles in Nashville were of the safety design. "As an evidence of their decadence in popularity it need only be stated that, although there are still more ordinaries than safeties in Nashville, the latter outnumber the former two to one when runs are made, showing that the practical features of the low style make it possible to ride on all occasions and over any sort of road, while the owner of the high machine stays at home and bewails the condition of the roads which might endanger his neck."[145]

According to one comparison:

*The advantage of the pony* [or safety] *over the "tall hoss" has been well illustrated on several occasions of late, notably upon recent runs over the Dickerson pike. There are several long hills on this pike, and recent rains and much travel have loosened the gravel with which it is paved, make it quite uncomfortable, to say nothing of the danger to coast them at full speed on an ordinary. Both wheels start together at the top. The ordinary rider, if he have common caution and regard for the preservation of his anatomy, will take a moderate pace, keeping a firm grip upon his bike, while the safety riders will turn his wheel loose, feeling perfectly secure, and reach the bottom hundreds of yards in from to his prejudiced friend, who is suspicious of an innovation. Reaching the level stretch at the bottom of the hill, Mr. Ordinary man has to expend much muscular force to regain his place beside his friend on the safety. This experience repeated a half dozen times on a twenty or thirty-mile trip must certainly tell severely on the ordinary rider, making a vast difference in the condition of the two when their destination is reached.*[146]

Despite the advantages of the safety design, the ordinary still had its devotees, particularly when riding in level, smooth country. While the ordinary was more dangerous a bike, it would never be deserted. "The graceful outlines we are so accustomed to seeing have, not as yet, been imparted to the safety, according to popular belief, although this may be pretty much a matter of education After the small wheel has been on the market longer and we become accustomed to seeing them their proportions will doubtless become as symmetrical too the average person as the other."[147] Non-wheelmen had an unjust belief that the safety, because of its smaller wheels, hadn't the ordinary's capacity for speed. But speed was determined by the gearing, not the wheel size. It was explained, "If one has a safety wheel geared to 60 inches, one revolution of the pedals will propel the wheel the same distance a high wheel 60 inches in diameter would go by one revolution of the pedals. This gearing gives increased friction, but the increased power obtained counter balanced this making the two styles of bikes about equal insofar as speed was concerned."[148] The "ordinary" had been perfected in 1886, when the more modern safety was, according to a newspaper article in the *Nashville American*, "far enough advanced toward perfection to make a bit for patronage, and the newcomer was not long in relegating the high wheel to the limbo of things discarded."[149] Reminiscing about his days on an ordinary bike, H.M. Doak, the editor of the *Nashville American*, said he had "knocked up a larger assortment of joints than my anatomical studies warranted me in believing could be found in the human frame by a series of 'headers.' I was skinned, barked, dislocated, confused and sprained to a shameful extent. In this plight I received notice of my election as honorary member

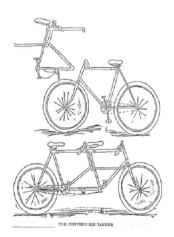

THE CONVERTIBLE TANDEM.

Conversion to a tandem bicycle. *Courtesy of the Tennessee State Library and Archives.*

of the Nashville Bicycle Club.…That was the day when the bold pioneer and adventurer mounted himself from thirty to sixty inches up in the air and took his life in his hands, or I might say, borrowing a metaphor from sporting circles, staked his life upon a turn of the wheel." In the earlier days of such cycling, the biker had not "forced himself upon the respect of the community, and Riding an Ordinary Bicycle. The Safety Bike with Pneumatic Tires nothing more delighted the driver of a market wagon than to turn square across the track, bringing about collision and destruction of forcing the unfortunate wheelman into gullies or upon direful headers."

"Those were the days of the genuine wheelman—I mean the pioneer days—a man with such pride in a glorious and adventurous past as the California '49ers takes in the past—compares with these effeminate days, when a new woman and even an old woman 'bikes as the old African lion hunter'…would compare lion hunting of his day with the tame sport of this time." Doak's views on the safety bike, considered by some as effeminate, had changed a great deal, and after eighteen years, he found that he would ride a safety bike, "and the safetyer [sic] the better." He traced the evolution of the bicycle from the velocipede in France, which was not much different from the current safety bike. A velocipede school was opened in Nashville, between Cherry Street and the square, but velocipiding was too awkward, and the ordinary bike offered more speed and balance to the sport. The ordinary, or "big wheel," was followed by a "little excuse for a wheel." As far as grace, the delight of motion, exhilaration and a sweet spice of danger are concerned, the world would never see the like of the big wheel.

> *Think of coasting down Paradise Ridge, legs over handle bars, a mile a second* [sic], *encountering, perhaps at the very bottom, a pebble of size such as never before hurt hair of human head…and taking a header of 40 feet through the air into a stone wall, and come up smiling, with only a few bruises, sprains, contusions, dislocated limbs, broken head and a wheel to carry back, a pleasant walk to town! That was the spice of wheel life! Only great sprits mounted the wheel in those days.*
>
> [Velociping] *was not a crime it could scarcely be called a vice; but it was a very awkward proceeding. I think a lofty sense of honor would condemn it as an unseemly thing. It was safe, with respect to that sort of cataclysmic disturbance, which as seemed inevitable with the latter high wheel, but the devotee sacrificed his self-respect, the respect of his neighbors, and died at somewhere between one and two years of nervous exhaustion— unless he reformed—and I think all of them reformed after about two*

*weeks' practice. I heard of no deaths.[150] A boy always learns to ride at once…because he commonly has no fear of breaking either himself or the machine; while a man may require anywhere from one lesson to a series that extend over weeks before he is really able to use his wheel on the road; just in proportion as he is fearless of disaster and can grasp the essential points that he does not need to balance the bicycle but only allow the bicycle to balance him without interference on his part.[151]*

It was a gradual process by which an ordinary or safety wheelman could work up to a fifty- or sixty-mile run each day without serious fatigue. "To become a racing man of any account, or even a 'road scorcher,' one must be both physically and mentally somewhat a phenomenon and the honor is not a very satisfactory one at best."[152] Yet cycling was more than just exercise or a sport. The danger involved in riding an ordinary bike "is one of the best features of the sport. Free from all elements of brutality it yet stirs up sluggish blood in a way all of us need sometimes, and the necessity of watch of cares engrosses the mind as to take it away from business cares.[153] When a man has learned to ride so well that he can extend his tours freely and gain distraction through freshness of surroundings, he can afford to try a safety or even a tricycle, but not profitably before."[154] Yet the growth of the sport depended not just on the bike in question or in cleansing one's mind from everyday cares; it also depended on good roads.

The so-called Good Roads movement was, in many ways, a result of bicycling advocates in the League of American Wheelmen (LAW).[155] In fact, the "father of good roads," Horatio Earle, acknowledged the connection in his 1929 biography. "I often hear nowadays the automobile instigated the good roads; that the automobile is the parent of good roads. Well, the truth is the bicycle is the father of the good roads movement.…The League [of American Wheelmen] fought for the privilege of building bicycle paths along the side of public highways. The League fought for equal privileges with horse drawn vehicles. All these battles were won and the bicyclist was afforded equal rights with other uses of highways and streets."[156] Indeed, without good roads, the bicycle would have remained a largely urban phenomenon, never able to venture from the confines of cities and towns. The clamor for good roads was heard at Vanderbilt University, which, taking "a hint from cyclists about improvement of highways," established a department of instruction in public highway construction in 1888.[157]

By January 1889, the LAW claimed 117 members in Nashville, where they enjoyed better conditions on Summer Street from Church Street to

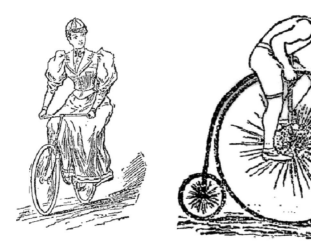

*Left*: Proper feminine bicycling attire in the late Victorian age. *Right*: A typical big wheel cyclist. *Library of Congress.*

Union Street. According to a story in the *Nashville American* titled "They Ride Silent Steeds," the unusually mild winter saw cyclists taking advantage of it, and "the average wheelman hailed with delight the presence of the city scavenger force on Church Street last week." Additionally, "repairs are being made on many streets in the city, and although the fresh rock make them bad for cycling now, they will be in fine condition by spring, it is hoped." Gravel, then as now, was a hazard for cyclists. January 13, 1889, promised to be "bright and will be taken advantage of by a large number of [cyclists] to participate in the regular 2:30 run, which will cover a new route—out the Gallatin Pike as far as the county farm. All wheelmen are requested to be at the club rooms at 2:15 o'clock."[158]

Nashville youth apparently did not, at first, take to bicycling as they did in other cities. This remained a mystery, but two reasons were suggested. First was the fear of personal injury to the uninitiated when learning to ride. The second was "that those who never enjoyed the sport are unable to truly appreciate the delights of a spin in the country."[159] Touring was a favorite pastime for amateur cyclists. For example, in June 1888, a group of wheelmen made a 130-mile tour from Nashville to Fayetteville in a riding time of fourteen hours. Likewise, a tour to Ashland City was planned.[160] A party of local wheelmen toured down to "Eldorado Springs Saturday afternoon."

*Their number was augmented by another party that went out on Sunday morning, the entire crowd coming back Sunday evening. Eldorado has always been a favorite with the boys, not only on account of the cool, shady bowers, the delightful waters, of which there are four or five different kinds, but more on account of the generous hospitality which is always extended them by the proprietor, Dr. Connell. He knows that a good appetite naturally follows indulgence in cycling, and his success in appeasing these ravenous demands…very naturally creates among wheelmen a kindly feeling for the Doctor, and hence it is they are always glad to go to Eldorado.*[161]

Of a greater distance was the tour taken on by four Nashville ordinary cyclists from the City of Rocks to Windsor, Ontario, Canada. Many doubted such an extended tour was even possible, yet it was successfully undertaken in 1887. The trip began in Nashville and then traveled to Louisville, Kentucky, in which a new speed record was set. From Louisville, the four set their sights for Bowling Green, and then went to Shelbyville, Kentucky; Frankfort, Kentucky; Florence, Kentucky; Cincinnati, Ohio; and then through Ohio to Buffalo, New York. Then they went across to Hamilton, Windsor, Ontario, Canada, and then to Detroit. From Detroit, they returned to Nashville via train, having traveled 640 miles in nine actual touring days, according to a Butcher hub cyclometer.[162] They averaged 71 miles per day. According to one newspaper article in 1888:

*Interest in cycling matters has risen…to the position of enthusiasm, the American desires to suggest to the management of the West Side Park the feasibility of adding to its already fine list of attraction for the fall fair a bicycle race. A number of local wheelmen to whom the matter has been mentioned by [wheelmen] have signified their willingness to participate in the contest should the fair management decide to arrange the races as a part of the program. The rules of the League of American Wheelmen prohibit competitive contests for a cash consideration, hence the prizes to offered would not be a matter of great financial outlay for the management. The first prize might be a new bicycle, the second a gold medal, and the third as cyclometer.…Or there might be two or three races arranged, of different classes, with medal prizes to be competed for. There is nothing more exciting than a closely contested race between expert wheelmen.*[163] *The enthusiastic interest of race between queens and king of the turf would hardly exceed that of the trial of speed and endurance between the riders of the silent steed. It would certainly be a big drawing card for the fair, and would be witnessed by hundreds who have not been permitted to see so novel an entertainment in Nashville.*[164]

And there were local races but none yet at the annual fair. For example, local races, such as the 1889 run to Franklin, demonstrated that "cycling is more talked of and more indulged in now in Nashville than ever before and a road race this fall would be a fitting finale to a season's sport."[165] In 1889, the Tennessee division of LAW met in Nashville. The parade committee of the local branch established the line of march for an expected mass of local and visiting wheelmen. The Committee on Runs established a four-day tour, from Nashville to Eagleville; Eagleville to Fayetteville; "over the short route" from Fayetteville to Lynchburg; Lynchburg to Shelbyville; Shelbyville to Lebanon, via Murfreesboro; and, finally, Lebanon to Nashville, covering a total of 201 miles.[166] The bikes in question were the high wheel type, although it seems likely that both were utilized.

In any event, the roads were capable of supporting the touring wheelmen. Fifteen cyclists, representing Nashville, Chattanooga, Memphis and Clarksville, were to race from the junction of Chestnut Street in South Nashville along the Lebanon Pike on "a contest of speed and endurance from here to Lebanon." The contestants had been in Nashville for a week, making practice runs to Lebanon before the race. Younger and inexperienced riders were handicapped, and there were a total of sixteen entries.[167]

*These entries represent some of the best riders in the state, and there is no doubt the stimulus of local pride, to say nothing of the valuable prizes to be won, will be an incentive to vigorous exertion on the part of each of the contestants to cross the wire first. The roads are in good condition, and there is no reason why the distance should not be made in good time. The last five miles of the route is as level as a racetrack, and as it is here the real contest will be, those who go will be as excitingly entertained as they would at a closely contested race.*[168]

At the race, Clarksville favorite Jeff Hearndon, the winner, rode a fifty-six-inch Victor; other ordinary bike brand names included a fifty-three-inch Newstar, a fifty-three-inch New Mail, a fifty-two-inch Club, a fifty-inch Light Champion and a Columbia Light Roadster. Riders were handicapped according to ability and past records and left the starting line at intervals of two minutes. Two wheelmen had gone over the course to guarantee that all the toll gates would be open to clear the track for the race.[169] A special train took fans to Lebanon to witness the finish of what promised to be an interesting and exciting race. "The merit of the various contestants was the subject of animated discussion among all the passengers." Hearndon was the "sho' winner." He was probably under twenty years old, weighed but 115 pounds and rode a fifty-six-inch wheel. "He was the winner of three events in 1887 and had not yet been beaten."[170] A newspaper story on July 2, 1888, titled "That Big Century Run" told how three Nashville cyclists, riding a fifty-six-inch New Mail, a fifty-three-inch New Mail and a fifty-inch New Rapid (all ordinary bicycles) left the city "over a part of the proposed route of 'the straight away century run' of the Nashville Bicycle Club, which is called for on July 4." The roads were in good condition when they left the public square at 3:32 a.m., and they arrived in Lebanon, thirty-one and a half miles away, at 6:50 a.m. and had their breakfast. After an hour's rest, "they mounted their wheels and reached Murfreesboro, twenty-six and a half miles away, "stopping only for a half hour's rest" before reaching Eagleville, eighteen and a half miles away, at 1:30 p.m. After lunch, they slowed down somewhat, passing through Triune and Nolensville at 4:40 p.m.

They arrived at the Nashville Customhouse at 7:30 p.m., having ridden 108 miles in twelve hours. Their average speed, including stops, was 9 miles per hour. Excluding stops, they averaged 10.8 miles per hour. This century marked the first time a "straight away run of over 100 miles has been made in the State, though they are common in sections of the country having better roads with fewer hills. All parts of the route had previously been wheeled over several times by one of the party and each time measured

The Start.

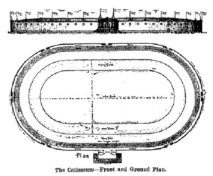

The Colisseum—Front and Ground Plan.

*Left*: Nashville fairgrounds where bicycle races were held. *Courtesy of the Tennessee State Library and Archives.*

*Above*: Nashville Coliseum. *Courtesy of the Tennessee State Library and Archives.*

by a Butcher hub cyclometer. The hub cyclometers in the party…registered over 108 miles, so there is little reason to doubt the distance."[171] While the century's contestants were accomplished using the ordinary bicycles, there were dangers in riding them. In fact, the dangers inherent in high wheel bicycling were believed to be a danger that only men could and should face. This helped—within the concept of the external artifactual context—keep cycling a masculine activity. Knowing what wheelmen found irksome tells us something of the difficulties they faced. For example, riders of ordinary bikes had a number of things they did not like. "Among them," according to an 1888 newspaper article, were:

Touring in the country. *Courtesy of the Tennessee State Library and Archives.*

*Headers. Street Sprinklers. Gutters across the sidewalk. To be laughed at when he takes a header. To be between streetcar rails two inches high on each side with a streetcar bearing down upon him and a crowd of pretty school girls watching him from the pavement. To be coasting down a hill, just wide enough for two vehicles, with rocks on each side, and coming around a curve, discover two vehicles standing in the middle of the road, the owners discussing politics. To have two street gamins, while his wheels is leaning against a fence, playing with the pedals, each one wagering that his will run the longest. To be climbing a steep hill, and just as he is looking at an inviting turn just ahead, to discover when he gets there that he is only one-third the way up. To be coasting down a steep hill at the rate of about fifteen miles an hour, and to suddenly see a lumber wagon about thirty feet long, with four mules attached, pop out across a lane about thirty yards ahead. To depend on a friend meeting him at a country town with the "stuff" to pay for a night's lodging and for him not to show up. To be toiling up a hill that has about one-fourth a mile more of backbone, with a wagon-load of girls coming up behind him, while his breath is already as far ahead that he can catch it only now and then, and he finds that he was born tired.*

Another pet peeve of cycling enthusiasts was the "road hog." According to a comment in the *Nashville American*, in April 1890:

*There are very few full-fledged "roadhogs" around Nashville. "Road-hog," in the vernacular of the wheel, is the man who is out for a drive and wants to monopolize the whole turnpike, forcing the unfortunate cyclist to take his chances with the rough places and rock piles on the roadside. Of course there are some, but a majority of people who are constant drivers on the pikes and streets show some regard for the safety of wheelmen by dividing the road with them. I had an experience with one of these fellows once that will never be forgotten, and which will be brought aginst [sic] him at the judgment day. It was when I was first learning to ride, and was out for a short run on a pike which had just received a fresh supply of stone. He doubtless saw, by the awkward manner in which I rode, that I was a beginner, and so he conclude to have some "fun" at my expense, and deliberately crowded me out into a pile of rock where I took the worst header of a lifetime. He was "sorry," of course, but that did not help me any. But there is a sequel to this. The same man can now be met almost any day out on the [roads], and he drives a horse that would rather walk over a circular saw than pass a wheel. And so it is always with grim satisfaction that I meet him now and send his horse dancing and buckjumping to the other side of the road, often requiring his best effort to avoid a runaway. The tables have been turned and I now have better control of my horse than he has of his.*

Bicyclists also were not afraid to flex their political muscles in local contests.[179] Two issues were up for debate: the trouble cyclists encountered with street sprinkling and the lantern law for nighttime riding. What they wanted was a blanket coverage of all vehicles for use of a lantern, not just bikers, and for the public works department to "leave a part of the streets unsprinkled for the benefit of bicyclists." Muddy streets were a hazard to the cycling enthusiast. According to a note in the newspaper: "Several years ago, the bicycle craze was at its height, but it has subsided to almost nothing…[because of] the lack of interest in riding through the wet streets after the spring carts have gone through."[173] One letter broadly hinted that there was a political quid pro quo in the balance. The "2,000 or more wheelmen in this city, by voting for the reform ticket, did no little towards assisting in the election of that ticket. There is no reason why the sprinkling question cannot be regulated satisfactorily to all classes of citizens."[174]

Indeed, bicycle manufacturing appeared in Nashville. In 1895, it was reported:

*The bicycle business is enlarging every day and during the past week a very large store-room has been opened at the stand formerly occupied by Buckner & Co., as a wholesale dry goods house. The entire first floor is filled with bicycles.*

*Another indication of larger trade expected is the probably establishment here of one of the largest bicycle factories in the country. A leading firm of wagon-makers made half a dozen bicycles as an experiment, and because of that experiment decided to try and organize the bicycle factory. So far everything is favorable, but the ultimate conclusion has not been arrived at. Negotiations are in progress with the man who has been the foreman in a factory where one of the very best bicycles in the world is manufactured. Only the most experienced talent will be engaged in the factory, and it is contemplated to turn out a wheel that is not exceeded by any now on the market.*[175]

The ordinary was not for women. Victorian social taboos restrained women from using such bicycles. The big wheel and women were opposing poles, regardless of split skirts or other bifurcated garments. Women, however, wanted to ride, and human ingenuity couldn't invent a side-saddle bike. When men found that women couldn't go with them on the "big wheel he invented the safety. Like everything modern," wrote one social commentator. "[The safety] is effeminate, luxurious, and degenerate, but it has come to stay."[176] Thus, bicycling, following the advent of the safety, was a permanent fixture in the social landscape, its use crossing gender lines. It even helped advance the movement for women's equality. No less of a leader in the movement for women's rights than Susan B. Anthony remarked, "Let me tell you what I think of bicycling. I think it has done more to emancipate women than anything else in the world. It gives women a feeling of freedom and self-reliance. I stand and rejoice every time I see a woman ride by on a wheel.…The picture of free, untrammeled womanhood."[177] Indeed, by 1888, the prejudice that cycling in Nashville was thought to be a recreation for men only had "in the past two or three years [had changed], and especial[ly] since the lighter and more improved tricycles have been placed on the market, many women…have been made 'converts' and now would not give up the exercise."[178] This was truer of cities in the East and North, but, claimed one local newspaper writer, the safety bike made it possible for women to exercise and even travel greater distances than ordinary male bikes. "'Bicycling was [accompanied]…largely on the devising and wearing of a becoming costume.' There it is again, the question of clothes. Isn't it queer how they must be inevitably and invariably considered wherever a woman is concerned?"[179] In 1888, it was predicted that women would soon be joining the cycling crowd by

*riding bicycles instead of the three wheeled vehicles which has formerly served them. What would be thought to see a lady riding a tricycle on the*

*Left*: Proper Victorian-era attire for women riding bicycles. *Library of Congress*.

*Below*: Satire of the new bicycling woman. *Library of Congress*.

*streets of Nashville? It would excite as much curiosity as is manifested by a youth from the rural districts upon his first visit to a metropolis. Yet, such a sight may be witnessed soon. A well-known young lady of one of our best families, living a short distance out on one of the pikes, has been negotiating with a local agent for a tricycle. As she is a pupil at one of our city schools, and if the purchase is made, and if it will be used by her to ride to and from school, thus serving as a very useful possession as well as a source of much health-giving and invigorating exercise. Custom is a wonderfully tenacious thing, and all that is necessary for the introduction of these machines for the use of ladies, is for someone to break the ice.... When it is demonstrated that this form of exercise is really more healthful than horseback riding, and may be indulged in without a possibility of modesty being outraged, the young ladies may not be slow to take it up.*[180]

While one woman had been taught to ride by her husband in 1889, masculine concerns about feminine modesty still manifested.

*There is a mistaken popular belief among those who have not seen a lady mounted on a wheel*[181] *that she must of necessity lay herself liable to an immodest exposure of ankles. This is of course, not the case, or cycling for ladies would not have become so popular in the East where ladies of the best families indulge in it. The ladies' wheel is so constructed that she sits on the saddle about like a person would sit on the corner of a table. There is no obstruction whatever from the saddle to her feet, the frame connecting the front and rear wheels, being what is called a drop frame. The only thing visible to the bystander is the down beneath the skirt in its work of propulsion. Any ordinary street dress may be worn by the rider, the idea being to obtain a garment as cool as possible. Female cyclists, now so much of a novelty here, will be so numerous next season as to cease to attract more than a passing notice, and then you may expect a boom in cycling for the young fellows never seen before.*[182]

Just two years later, 1891, a newspaper report held that women were concerned about feminine bike riding. It "might not be generally known, but there are scores of ladies right here in Nashville who are anxious to keep pace with the times, as their Northern, Western and Eastern sisters are doing, and acquire the sixth sense—that of cycling. They are kept back generally by their fathers, brothers, or others, who never having ridden, know nothing of a thing can be usually do give the most advice on the subject."[183] Male chauvinism thus worked to keep women off bicycles in Nashville. Riding a bicycle was no more scandalous than skating or tumbling. "It would appear," wrote one reporter, writing under the pseudonym "Billy Crank Turner," "that the healthfulness of wheeling for girls is established insofar as present experience goes."[184] By 1893, an illustration in the *American* titled "The Bicycle Girl" indicated what modesty demanded of female cyclists.

Along with predictions of a boom in bicycles in the summer of 1894, the *American* noted, "A number of well-known ladies have learned to ride bicycles….This summer there will be a large number of Nashville lady riders on Nashville streets."[185] Wearing apparel was still a topic of modesty for women, but if the split skirts popular in Paris and New York indicated anything, it was that solutions to the dilemma had been found. Yet it was pronounced that the "only dress that is suitable for a woman is one on the order of a horseback-riding costume, which, with the exception of the length, but very full. This makes a very modest and at the same time neat dress."[186] The pleasant weather of early May 1895 saw many young women learning to ride bicycles at the Vanderbilt grounds. It took only a day or two to learn. Nevertheless, "very few girls can mount or dismount gracefully; in fact these are the hardest points they have to overcome."[187] One woman writer, Clara Mai Howe, explained, "It is thought that it is only a question of time when the lady's wheel will be abolished and she will don her bloomers and ride a man's [ordinary bike]."

> Let's go slowly and suffer ourselves to be handicapped by the extra five pounds of weight and our skirts. The weight of the ladies' wheel could be somewhat reduced if we could do away with the mud guard, but that we cannot do so long as our streets are in the condition they are from improper sprinkling….That the "fad" for women to ride a wheel is daily gaining ground is an undisputed fact. Almost each hour sees new converts to cyclist. The tirade which was raised against the appetence of the "new belief" is rapidly subsiding, and a girl is not quite "fin de siècle" now unless she is a devotee of the wheel, whether she is the owner of one or not. Until riding becomes a "matter of course instead of discussion," there will still be those who still who will frown upon it. It is hoped that the millennium of wheeling will be hastened, and then, if ever, those who are now "groaning in darkness" will realize that "it is not all of life to live."

Bicycle racing enthusiast. *Library of Congress*.

*Watch the girls as they spin along. Do not their sparkling eyes, their rosy cheeks and their happy voices speak volumes of their enjoyment of life? Yet some of us deny our girls this innocent, healthy pleasure. Many object to cycling for women. Why? Simply because it is an innovation. Perhaps some fifty years ago it would have seemed rather strange for maidens to have used modern "spinning wheels." But this is a progressive urge, and we must keep abreast of the times. What would have been thought of our men half a century ago had they parted their hair "right in the middle" as is the present style? They would have been considered ridiculously absurd. When a man parts his hair in the middle, femininity does not rise up and declare that her rights have been infringed upon; neither can masculinity say that a woman approaches near the borders of his territory when she rides a wheel. Grandfathers, fathers, you who are sometimes cynically inclined to ask yourselves: "What is going to become of the girls of this age? What will they be doing next?" Away with such questions! Be assured that your granddaughters, your daughters, possess the same sweet, true, womanliness which made so dear to you that whispered "yes" of long ago. The incidence of female riders had increased to a time when "it was such a rarity that people ran to their doors to see one go by."[188]*

By May 1895, "the town is full of them and lady cycling clubs are all the rage, from which men are barred." Still, women did not go wheeling alone and generally had a male escort, yet "since they have multiplied in numbers they," echoing Clara Mai Howe's observation, "have grown more independent, and by getting together take fine spins out on the pike."[189] Clothing was still an issue, as on one outing, a mad horse charged a party of women cyclists, forcing them to abandon their bikes and take refuge behind a barbed wire fence. They all decided there "was nothing to compare with the bloomer costume worn by lady cyclists. The President [of the club] had shown just as much trepidation and fright as her seven members, and for a protector (i.e. male escort) wasn't worth a cent."[190] By July 1895:

*The new woman, with her up-to-date bloomers, has appeared in Nashville. You don't see her on the streets during business hours, nor is it a common occurrence to see her in the cool of the afternoon wheeling along the boulevard where so many cyclists congregate. But she is here, and once the "ice is broken," look out for more of them. She was out bright and early yesterday morning, so early indeed that but few were up to enjoy the sight. An American reporter, tired from his night's labor, was wending his way homeward just as the sun was beginning to tinge with a golden hue the fleecy clouds that were rapidly flying overhead, and but for his lonesome presence Church Street would have been deserted. Suddenly, from Spruce street's corner, a beautiful apparition burst into view and the reporter forgot his night of toil. The apparition was refreshing to a degree, and no more appreciative audience than that lone reporter could have been collected. What it lacked in numbers it made up in enthusiasm. There she was, attired in a natty check suit, the cutaway coat fitting her shapely shoulders and waist in a style that enthusiastic audience voted bewitching. Then if the coat was a perfect fit, the bloomers were more so. A pair of leggings, that blended easily with the checks of the trou-bloomers, reached up to her knees. A jaunty cap sat upon a wealth of golden hair, done up in a close compact style. From under her cap's brim peered a pair of lustrous blue eyes intent on the path before her. Altogether she was a delightful picture. Evidently out for a long run, she was moving with an ease and grace that bespoke of the expert, while her utter oblivion to outside affairs clearly demonstrated her devotion to the wheel. Otherwise, she would have noticed that fellow standing on the sidewalk with "admiration" spelt in every lineament of his countenance. She didn't, though, much to his chagrin, and she disappointed further up the street, gliding gracefully around another corner. There may have been some lucky fellow accompanying that fair vision, somewhere back in the rear. The reporter is not prepared to testify on this point, but he thinks maybe he did catch a glimpse of some insignificant-looking figure following along in the wake of the vision he told you of.*[191]

Tandem bikes became increasingly popular, allowing an escort to ride the same bike as the woman cyclist. The number of women cyclists, notwithstanding the popularity of the "bicycle built for two," had more than trebled, judging from "the number of women's wheels local dealers are selling." The tandem, or bicycle built for two, made its appearance as well. One West End gentleman was known to have no trouble finding a woman to ride with him on his tandem. One prominent Nashville dealer told a reporter that in the previous year, he had only nine women's cycles, and in 1896, fully thirty-two and that at the beginning of the season, "Other dealers are also selling more of this kind of wheel than ever before, and the Nashville public will see many fair cyclists on the streets and boulevards during the long afternoons this summer."

However, one "well-known practitioner of considerable repute" had bad things to say about women and bicycling. It was her declaration that the effects of the exercise were injurious to the lady rider. "The physician further remarked that she does not ride a wheel and never has." One of the physician's well-known feminine acquaintances was in hearing distance when the wheel was so dismissed and "immediately exclaimed: "Why, Doctor, I am sure you are wrong in the matter. I have ridden for three years now and never experienced any of the effects of which you speak. I am sure that every woman in America would become stronger and healthier were she to adopt wheeling for the recreation this exercise gives."[192] A good epitome of the rise and prominence of women cyclists in nineteenth-century Nashville is found in an April 12, 1896 *Nashville American* article titled "THE FAIR BICYCLE GIRL." According to the story:

*WITH THE BLOSSOMING OF THE SPRING SHE BLOOMS SHE COMES DOWN THE SUNLIGHT ROAD WITH ROSES IN HER CHEEKS AND SUNSHINE IN HER EYES—THE LADY RIDERS OF NASHVILLE, THEIR WHEELS AND CLUBS. With the blossoming of the flowers the bicycle girl blooms forth. She comes down the sunlight road with roses caught on her cheek and sunshine in her eyes, and as she speeds along the highways, exhilarated and happy, I give to her and her dearest fad a rising toast: "May she, like the flowers, live under the bluest skies and amid the balmiest surroundings; may she never fade, but with their 'bike' defy ill health and old age."*

*A seller of bicycles asserted the other day that there was $500,000 invested in wheels in Nashville. When one considers that 1,000 ladies own wheels this seems probable. At first nearly all the physicians declared wheels to be injurious to women, and so the timid of the sex let go and the stronger sisters rode on. At the end of the season the girl with the rosiest cheeks and strongest muscle was she who had mounted this unique invention and glided to green pastures. The athletic women, in whatsoever guise she comes, should be welcomed; for she is sure to be a healthy, agreeable companion. Fragile women with languishing, tender, sentimental moods are almost sure to have bad digestive organs and usually most tiresome dispositions. So, many of them torment themselves to a remarkable degree by morbidly taking hold of somebody's shortcomings and brooding over them, when really the trouble is the lack of fresh air and exercise. Put that woman on a wheel, speed her to the country, and she returns bright and cheerful, having forgotten altogether the animated discussion at breakfast when man seemed unendurable.*

*"Between the X rays and the bicycle," enthusiastically declared Miss Frances Willard in Chicago the other day, "the temperance women will find their vocation gone in fifty years. The X rays will take interior views of a man and conclusively prove to him the evil effects of alcohol and nicotine and the wheel will do the rest. The fact is modern inventions are doing a great ethical work not adequately appreciated." Mrs. Rover, whom the ladies in this city seemed to heartily indorse, declared the wheel a salvation to women. The beautiful country surrounding our city affords an unending delight to the wheelers. The favorite runs are out the boulevard by Melrose and out the Franklin road. The High Bridge, returning the White's Creek road, gives the sixteen-mile spin that the best riders enjoy. The Harding road is a popular road also. These lovely spring afternoons bring out hundreds of riders, and among them some of our most prominent young women, who declare there is no sport half as enjoyable. One enthusiast said her health had been infinitely better since riding the wheel, and if women would only wheel more all of their ills would vanish. "You must be a connoisseur, though," she said, "to get the best result. Of course you would never wheel up hill. It affects the heart, and unless has great strength it should not be attempted. The position taken in riding is a most important feature. Sit erect; keep knees together, and do not crook the elbows." This young woman, who looks most attractive on her wheel, declared bloomers an abomination. "Not only are the unsightly, but they are not even as convenient as the short skirt." The sterner sex will all want to shake hands with this girl, but she expresses the sentiment of thousands of women, which has been so strong on this subject that even extremists now announce the short skirt the correct costume. "Never try to coast on a cheap wheel," she continued. "You never know the weak part, and in coasting something is apt to break and off you go." An important improvement, it is said, will soon be made in the saddle of the bicycles. One of the complaints made by physicians is that the seats are too small and improperly constructed. The bicycle manufacturers have been quick to recognize these defects, and during the present season especially the market is supplied with saddles that avoid most of the dangers that old saddles gave rise to. Women are especially warned against the hard, long saddle. To obviate this special pads are in the market which could be affixed by a strap to any seat. Altogether there are said to be about 3,000 ladies who ride the wheel in this city, and 8,000 riders including gentlemen. There are several bicycle clubs in the city. There is a West End Cycling Club, composed of a number of young men and…ladies…[list follows]. There is a cycling club at Ward's Seminary, composed of eighteen of the boarders.*

Tillie Anderson, U.S. female cycling champion. *Courtesy of the Tennessee State Library and Archives.*

*These young women wear suits the color of the college uniform, and with the college colors in ribbons, caught with college pins make an attractive display. Prof. Blanton usually accompanies them. A number of younger [women], who are excellent cyclists, have a club which meets every Friday afternoon. They are enthusiasts and make long runs.[193]*

There were likewise some problems associated with bicycling in Nashville. One newspaper story titled "The New Cyclists" exposed some nagging problems.

*Dealers may well warn new cyclists against the habits complained of… since nothing trends more to bring the sport into disrepute with the better people than the reckless riding indulged in by these thoughtless riders. The complaint may also be made in Nashville with justice. Numerous complaints have been received, and many instances are continually being reported as to the result of reckless riding on the part of the "new cyclist." Much has already been said on the subject, but not enough, seemingly, to check the bone breaking scorcher. Who of late has been very much in evidence on riverside drive and other good cycling thoroughfares uptown. "The new cyclist" is either [a] bloomerclad wheel woman or a youth of uncertain age, who has just learned to ride, in addition thereto has mastered the "art" of gliding along "without hands."*

*In nine cases out of ten these youths own a conspicuous Golf suit, and go about mounted on hired wheels. They, of course, have acquired a "mastery" in some cycling academy, and are "expert" riders, but their knowledge of the laws of the road would do credit to a 5-year old child. They go tearing up and down the avenues as if their lives depended upon it, never stopping to think that whether they are on the right or left side or that there are others about them, with the result that it is really dangerous for a wheelman of peaceful mind to venture out in broad daylight, to say nothing of the night…women…[who] are the principal offenders against the laws of the road. They ride on any side of the street that is, best to their liking, and keep wheelmen who keep within the limits of the law in a state of constant anxiety, as it is impossible to tell which way the fancy of the fair devotees will take them.[194]*

Bicycle races were, at first, affairs carried out on the high wheel bicycle, and racers themselves "were less than enthusiastic about the invention of the chain-drive bicycle, which brought riders down off the dangerous high wheels of the ordinary bikes." The daredevil image of the riders who were brave enough to pedal fast on high wheelers was in jeopardy. Then with the invention of air-filled pneumatic tires, bicycles suddenly became more comfortable. Again, the rugged image of cyclists was threatened by the notion that bicycle riding could actually be pleasant. Within a few years, though, as it became clear that the new inventions not only made cycling safer and more comfortable but also faster and more efficient, racers embraced the pneumatic tire safety bike. As bike racing began to become popular in America, bike races themselves became professional, long and more of an entertainment spectacle.[195] In American cities, the sport led to the construction of racetracks; in the case of Nashville, the Coliseum was built in 1895.[196] By May 1896, the management of the Coliseum had arranged for "professional bicycle races to begin." Professional bicyclists were followed as closely as baseball teams and rivaled baseball as a sports pastime.[197]

Bicycle racing, in its first manifestation, was primarily a matter for local bicycle clubs, usually utilizing an ordinary bike on public roads. For example, a proposed seventeen-mile race was announced in 1891, from Nashville to Franklin, along with other events for safety and high wheel bikes. Twenty-six entries were made, ten from Nashville and five from as far away as Memphis—there was even a Clarksville contestant. The races were for both types of bikes, but during the race to Franklin, pneumatic cushion tire wheels and pneumatics were to be penalized per minute.[198] In any event, bicycle races came to be so popular that a facility was built solely for their exhibition. By October 1895, the Nashville Coliseum was scheduled for completion, allowing for races along a track. It was touted as "one of the institutions of the city when completed....It will contain nine thousand seats and the floor is built so that it can be taken up and put down as required." While it allowed for athletic events from Olympic style contests to football, it was intended mainly for bicycle races. The track was "eight laps to the mile," built in the most substantial manner and according to the latest ideas on a scientific plan "that will make it not only the largest and fastest track in the world." On opening night, after other athletic events, there was to be an "eighteen-hour bicycle race for the championship of the State, three hours each night for six nights. By that time there will be a large number of crack riders here and an international tournament will be given, in which the crack riders of the world will participate."[199]

As racing's popularity grew in the United States and Nashville, "bike races became longer and more of an entertainment spectacle." Indeed, the most outstanding racing event of all was the six-day race, which caught on in America around 1890. Held in racing coliseums, cyclists would ride around the tracks for six days. Earlier races entailed cyclists to ride an exhausting 18 hours a day, the contest soon slipping into an uninterrupted 144-hour debacle. "Cyclists were pushed well beyond the point of exhaustion, while bands played in the infield, gambling ran wild, and gawkers filled the grandstands hoping for the chance…to see one of the racers collapse and crash to the ground."[200]

The day before its grand opening, the Coliseum was the scene where professional cyclists, practicing for the big event, "SMASHED THE RECORDS."

> *The fact that there is to be a race between eight champions for the twelve-hour record of the United States should alone be sufficient to make the attendance something phenomenal. When the fact is added that each one of these eight contestants has a record of less than two minutes for a mile, and that this is the first time there has been such a race with eight contestants, there should be wonderful interest. The great twelve hour race will be run two hours each night for six nights. The remaining time will be taken up to other sports and races. Every night there will be contests for the local champions in the amateur and professional classes.*

Many professional records were set in Nashville. For example, Mr. Barnet "[has] all the time contended that this track would be the fastest indoor track in the world.….[He] yesterday went two laps on the new track in 21 seconds, a 1:35 gait, and faster than any record ever made heretofore in the world.….The mile yesterday was within a second of the fastest mile made on a straightaway track. This record was made on the boulevard at Buffalo on the quad last August." Tandem records were met or exceeded at the Coliseum.[201] Any amateurs, according to LAW regulations, lost their status as amateurs if they participated in a race with professionals.[202] The Coliseum held professional races from 1895 to 1897, three or four times a year. Many local cyclists "gained fame as speedy pedal pushers.…Tennessee boys from this section who…proved the possession of speed on the bike." Bankruptcy forced the coliseum to remain unused until 1901, when it was reused for horse shows. By 1904, it was demolished.[203]

Perhaps surprisingly, women also competed for national records at the Nashville Coliseum, particularly Tillie Anderson, who raced against the French national women's title holder Mille Lisette. They raced for the World's Women's Championship in 1899 at the Coliseum in a ten-hour competition.[204] In 1900, there was a six-day race at the Coliseum, with some of the most famous names in the business. The main event in 1900 for the "lady championship of America" was the race between Lisette and Anderson. The latter upheld her championship. Other races were held for other women's records, with Tillie Anderson usually the winner. Consider a wide variety of reform efforts that engaged progressive women in Tennessee before, after and during the suffrage movement. Evins demonstrates Tennessee women's engagement with politics long before they had the vote, ran for office or served on juries and supports the argument that a broader definition of "politics" permits a fuller incorporation of women's public activities into U.S. political history.

# 5

# WHAT THE BOYS READ

On June 17, 1882, the *Nashville Daily American* included a rare human interest story decrying "trashy literature" and its ruinous effects on the development of moral fiber and social conduct of juvenile boys. Such ten-cent reading material was judged a clear and present danger, leading youths to lives of depraved crime and dissipated ruin. Because the First Amendment prohibited any law that sought to suppress the printing of such "dime novels," it was the responsibility of parents to curb the reading of such outrageous literature and align their sons on the proper path to moral redemption. The tone of the following newspaper article is reminiscent of some contemporary claims that video and role-playing games corrupt young minds. It was titled "WHAT THE BOYS READ."

*The Glorification of Crime and the Depraving of Youth. The Trashy Effects which Daily Corrupt the Morals of the Young. Among all the fruitful causes of frightful depravity of today among the boys and youths of our country there is none more potent than the trashy literature which floods the country and which is supplied by every newsstand in every city to feed the morbid appetite of it votaries. The reading of it is not an exception, but a rule, and the boys of parents able to furnish better mental food are the more addicted to it, because they possess the greater means to procure it. In this day of cheap reading, when almost all the finest specimens of modern and older fiction can be procured at such a low cost, there is no reason why every family where there are boys cannot be furnished with healthful, wholesome reading. When ten cents will buy a work that our fathers could only procure at twenty times the cost, there is no excuse for the extensive circulation of the vile trash published by New York firms, whose sole object must be to deprave human nature by the publication of the worst "rot" that could be imagined. It may be said that this stuff is cheap, but it is not cheap; it is printed on the coarsest, dirtiest papier and illustrated with the coarsest pictures. In all this line of papers "for boys and young gentlemen" there is never published a story the hero of which is respectable, and never printed a picture that is not full of grossest caricatures and deformity. The hero is always young and noted for finding out in some sneaking manner the vile sins of his father, the rascality of his employer, by which he gets money and enjoys unheard-of privileges as a sort of blackmail. None of these boys follow any respectable business or any honorable occupation. They are young pirates, ruffians and blacklegs, and their careers are written with the devilish ear that lures the young and silly reader of them into emulating their deeds. Parents are always harsh and unjust, schools are prison houses of cruelty and the teachers are invariably tyrants who have no affection whatever for the boys and rarely a single redeeming trait of character, unless he sides with the boys, runs away with them from school and becomes a vagabond, wandering over the world, dead-beating his way in impossible manners, thrashing out hordes of banditti and entire tribes of Indians by the most remarkable methods. Outlawry is glorified and murder forms so large a part of these stories that it is no wonder that some such cases occur as that of the boy of fourteen who was lynched for cold-blooded assassination a few days ago in Minnesota. Emulation of the characters in the trashy stories he had been reading he assigned as the reason of his deed. How many homes are daily saddened and how many lives blighted and ruined, how many fond hopes crushed, but the results of reading the infamous publications of such firms as those referred to. As said above, these papers are not cheap, for the same amount of money would buy a larger quantity of reading mater, well primed and calculated to improve instead of vitiating the taste. Take the "libraries." These villainous publications contain sixteen pages of vile printing, and are sold for a nickel. The standard "libraries," published by reputable firms, are larger in page, and ten cents buys one containing forty or even sixty or more pages. They embrace history, biography travel and adventure, scientific subjects, wit, humor, poetry, fiction—every class of literature. The contents of the others can be judged from their titles, samples of which, copied from the supplies of the stand of a Nashville newsdealer, are here given. Note the elegance of the titles:* Snoozer, the Boy Sharp; Evil Eye, the King of the Cattle Thieves; Capt. Apollo, the Kingpin of Bowie, or Flash o' Lightning's Feud; One-eyed Sim; Hawkeye Henry; Deadly Eye; Faro Frank; Old Effects Frosty; Vagabond Jo; The Boy Bedouins; The Boy Demon; The Boy Pards; Roving Jo, or the History of a Young Border Ruffian; Jack Hoyle, the Young Speculator, or the Road to Fortune; Sassy Sam, or a Bootblack's Voyage Around the World; Daddy Brush, Taken in and Done For; The Red Headed League. *These are fair samples of the whole lot. They can be seen on any news-stand, by anyone who imagines them gotten up for use in this article. The stories themselves are fairly gotten up to the titles. The titles give in every instance the heroes of the stories. From a single page in one of these stories are taken the following choice expressions, which indicate the style of conversation adopted: "Shut up; yar too fresh; go take salt"; "You arn't [sic] game"; "That's what I warble; yes, yer bet I weaken'"; "Give me another taste of the sucker"; "Joe learned of an old rooster, a naturalist"; "Yer a snide"; "I'm stuffed; full as a goat"; "Be gob [sic] I wud I wur a Nihilist." There are plenty more, but surely that is enough. And the sub-title of the sheet is, "An Entertaining and Instructive Journal for American Youths!" Ridiculous as all this may appear, it is a serious matter. Nothing but evil can possibly come of it. All sorts of crimes are condoned or justified, and the boys are quick to take the lesson. Newsdealers say that the boys who buy these things have to be watched all the time, and in spite of the closest watching, they still manage to steal them. Two or three days ago an American reporter was standing on the Maxwell House corner, when a boy, coming down Church Street with two of these papers, met a companion on the corner, who asked: "Did you get it?" "You bet." "What racket?" "Oh, the same old lay; one in the other." "He'll tumble to that and jump you; every other fellow has got on to that lay, and fag you." These boys were both of good family. Yet, one of these lads, depraved by the mental pabulum he stooped to steal, boasted of the act. Can it be remedied? may well be asked, and may well be doubted: After a youth arrives at the age when he has sense enough to see the falsity and the lowness of this stuff, there is no danger of his picking up a taste for it. But the young who begin reading it are depraved before they acquire sense enough to stop it, and turn out young vagabonds and loafers, familiar with all the ways of crime. The only remedy in which there is any hope is in more attention by parents to what their children are reading. Those who can read will read, and it is easy to direct the taste to a proper channel. With so many cheap and elegant publications as there are now seen on the stalls of newsdealers, there is no excuse for any family where there are children, being without good reading matter. Unless the parents take it in hand there is little hope of correcting the rapid spread of vicious reading and the crime that necessarily accompanies this increase. They must give it serious attention, not spasmodically, but continued, until there is some perceptible improvement; until cheek and effrontery are not looked upon by their boys as energy and independence; until indecency and the low dialect of rowdies and roughs do not pass for wit; until every paper that seeks to inflame the basest passions of human nature, to glorify crime and outlawry is forced to suspend, and when popular opinion will not suffer the purchase of a paper from the same counter where these villainous, poisonous and depraved periodicals are exposed for sale. Since there can be no law for their suppression, popular opinion must take the matter in hand. The traffic can be suppressed in this way, and the sooner it is done the fewer of the boys of this city and of this country will be sent to destruction by the perusal of this trashy literature.*

# THE AUGUSTUS KENNETH WARD FORGERY SCANDAL IN MEMPHIS

## *1895–1902*

*"Ward was flush with money and was in a hilarious mood."*

*I*n mid-October 1895, news of the forgeries, embezzlement and the flight of Augustus Kenneth "A.K." Ward, the general manager, secretary and treasurer of the Memphis Board and Heading Company, was beyond belief. Soon after he secretly absconded from Memphis, it was known beyond a doubt that he secured at least $200,000 on forged paper before his departure, $170,000 from local and out-of-state and local banks, brokers and moneylenders. The remaining $30,000 came from widows, orphans and personal friends. It was a fortune.

Being professedly a devout church member, Ward had a large, wide circle of acquaintances among the widows and orphans in Memphis. He had a reputation as a shrewd businessman, and more than a dozen widows thought it would be safe to place their money in his hands, and he left no opportunity to borrow escape his grasp. At first, his indebtedness paper was quoted at the ordinary rates of discount. Then as it became voluminous and fell into the hands of brokers—or rather was placed by him in their hands—the rates of discount went higher, and it was known that he secured some money with promises to pay as much as 15 percent on the debt.

Ward's forgery methods of operation were of his own invention. Sometimes, he forged only one name, and at other times, he forged as many as three or four. One of his schemes was to go to one of the men who had been endorsing for him with a joint note, get them to sign it and tell them that the other endorsers would do the same thing. Then he would forge the other names. The next not to be forged would be drawn up in the same way and taken to another, his signature obtained and the signatures of others forged. By the time Ward had gone around the circle, he would have a large sum of money, and each endorser would have knowledge by part of his borrowings. Ward would take each fraudulent note of this kind to the bank, where the genuine endorser did business, and the bankers, seeing this signature was all right, would naturally infer there was no trouble about the rest of the signatures.

The sudden death of S.A. Williamson, the largest stockholder of the successful Memphis Barrel and Heading Company and a wealthy businessman, caused the exposure and Ward's rushed departure from Memphis. When Williamson died, those who held notes with his forged name began to clamor for another endorser, and finding he could get none, Ward fled. Finding himself face to face with disgrace, he went to his wife, confessed his forgeries and told her he would have to leave the country. She agreed to share his fate, and together, they left for New Orleans on October 8. From there, they booked passage to Port Cortez, Belize, British Honduras, on October 14 on board the steamer *Breakwater*.

> *The comparison of notes by various interested parties showed that there was about $100,000 of forged paper in Memphis, the remainder being from other cities. Ward, as general manager of the Memphis Barrel & Heading Company, had authority such as managers have for legitimate uses. To what extent the firm was bound by Ward's embarrassing forgeries was a query that remained to be answered.*

It was learned that the Mechanics' National Bank of New York held $30,000 of the paper made by Ward with forged indorsements of reputable Memphis businessmen. Two other New York banks each held $10,000 worth of his fabricated debt. Additionally, two Chicago banks were in it for a total of $20,000, while private parties in Cincinnati, Saint Louis and New Orleans held the bogus paper in sums of $3,000 to $8,000. His victims made their appearances in court soon after learning of his absconding with so much cash, and by that evening, every piece of property in which he had an interest had been bound over and was in the hands of the sheriff.

A.K. Ward was a native of Nashville and had come to Memphis with several years prior. There, he began work as an attorney. Yet he was not successful in that endeavor and turned his attention to business. In that capacity, he was described as "energetic and nervous." As an entrepreneur, he made friends in the highest social and business circles of Memphis; their confidence in him was full-throated and affirmative. Ward settled in Memphis in the 1880s and led a double life faultlessly. He maintained a palatial mansion on the outskirts of the Bluff City on the Hernando Road. For all appearances, he was attentive to his wife. He was the superintendent of a Sunday school and was renowned as the loudest singer in the congregation. He gave freely to charity and was regarded as a model Christian man. At the same time, Ward, it was stated, "secretly maintained another residence in the city which has been the scene of many orgies." (There was no elaboration on this last commentary.)

Ward was a "veritable heavyweight in business, though light physically," having various irons in a number of fires. Before the scandal, he had a stellar reputation as an up-and-coming businessman, except, ironically, among a select circle of bankers who did not "care to handle his personal paper, even with a pair of tongs." Aside from being the superintendent of a Sunday school, he registered in society through his marriage to the daughter of S.H. Toof, a wealthy Memphis publisher. The wedding was judged to be "a great social event, large sums of money being spent in making it eclipse any other wedding in point of splendor that has occurred in Memphis in a long time." Mrs. Ward was a "pretty blonde" and was one of "the leaders of the local four hundred." Through such contacts, he became general manager of the Memphis Barrel and Heading Company.

After the elaborate wedding, Mr. Toof displayed great interest in his son-in-law and furnished him with money to start in business. It was soon apparent, however, that Ward was no manager, and he soon "ran through with the old man's shekels." Toof endorsed Ward's paper debt until it reached $15,000; then, he cut Ward off and refused to put up any more cash. This situation caused Ward to begin his forgery, which did not stop until he was discovered and forced to flee Memphis.

Ward, according to an article in the *Memphis Commercial Appeal*, was described as about "35 years old, five feet, eight inches tall, with small, piercing brown eyes, dark complexion; heavy brown mustache, light weight, and wears a round hat."

Through his social contacts, he became the general manger of the successful Memphis Board and Heading Company and secured the interest of several of the richest men in the city to invest in that concern, which grew to an even higher profitability. He managed plantations near Memphis and in Mississippi. After absconding with his loot and departing from New

Orleans, he headed to Port Cortez, Belize, British Honduras. "Ward," ran one report, "was flush with money and was in a hilarious mood." The amount of money the fugitive forger and embezzler made off with varied in estimates from $125,000 to no less than $300,000, both incredibly large sums of money in 1895. When the sensational news broke, and the full measure of his crimes was exposed, the city became aroused. There was "not a shadow of a doubt that if the angry populace could lay hands on Ward he would be hung to the nearest telephone pole. This feeling of indignation among the people was caused by the heartlessness and cold bloodiness, with which he deliberately robbed widows and orphans." He made a habit of watching the obituaries for the deaths of men who had their lives insured. His eagerness to get possession of the little legacies prompted him to begin plans soon after the funeral to "secure the widows' and orphans' money."

> *His standing in the church, the high rates of interest he offered and the gilt-edged forged endorsements enabled him to speedily engraft himself into the good graces of the widows and the money was promptly forthcoming… He…swindled eighteen widows in this manner in eight months.*

His short-lived career of theft and forgery was conducted with little thought of the impacts his dealings would entail, typical behavior for sociopaths. "The world was his 'oyster,' and victims were so many instruments" for his fraudulent accumulation of so much money. One widow was conned into lending Ward $2,500 "in one lump of counterfeit notes."[205]

Meanwhile, in Memphis, the Chancery Court was awash with petitions to force the Memphis Barrel and Heading Company to make good the sham, which was a grim mesh. It was revealed that the books of the company contained a plethora of forged entries, as well as a bogus resolution by the board of directors authorizing Ward to borrow money for the business. Moreover, Ward had torn pages from the minute book containing the corporation's by-laws and either destroyed or carried them with him. The accounts were in a "hopeless tangle, and hand or tails could not be made of them." While he and his spouse were sailing to Belize (or British Honduras), an effort was made to intercept the fugitive and bring him back to face charges in Memphis. Chief of Police Mosely was dispatched to Puerto Cortez, Belize, to intercept Ward and return him to Memphis. However, there was no treaty of extradition with Belize, no doubt a major reason why Ward chose that Central American colony as his getaway destination. Mosely was forced to track Ward throughout Central America.

The only way in which Mosley could hope to apprehend Ward without the aid of an American minister and consul at Honduras was to "kidnap the rascal…and the chances would be about even that Ward would kidnap Mosely."[206] It looked as though he had premeditated his egress with great care and that he would elude authorities and prosecution for his felonies.[207]

The chief's efforts were to no avail, owing to the lack of a treaty of extradition with Honduras. Consequently, the editors of the *Memphis Appeal* newspaper, who had loaned Ward $900, petitioned Governor Peter Turney for assistance in apprehending the fugitive. Turney, in turn, contacted United States secretary of state Richard Olney for his help in what was becoming an international affair.[208] There was no FBI to take the matter in hand.

Upon landing in Port Cortez, Belize, the *Breakwatrer*'s master went ashore and obtained from the American consulate a cable asking if Ward and his wife (using the alias Mr. and Mrs. August W. Kenneth) were still on board the ship. Yes, they were, but the ship was in port for just a few hours. While at Puerto Cortez, Honduras, the American Consul came aboard and provided the ship's captain a cable from the *Memphis Appeal* that furnished a litany of Ward's transgressions and asked that he be kept aboard ship. The consular agent immediately telegraphed to Tegucigalpa to the consul general for instructions and received a reply that, under the circumstances, it would be impossible to arrest him. The telegram came from a newspaper and was not an official United States Department of State notice. Mr. and Mrs. Ward left the vessel with their baggage and made their way to Tegucigalpa, Honduras, by rail.[209]

Ward landed in Puerto Cortez on October 16, 1895, and was soon residing in Tegucigalpa, the capital of the Republic of Honduras. It was reported that he was to take possession of a large land grant given him, some several hundred manzanas (about 1.7 acres each), by the contiguous Republic of Honduras, land he was allowed to select himself. He intended to grow Sea Island cotton and establish a cotton mill within three years. If he was successful in his plans, he would be granted another tract of land of the same size. He was also given the exclusive right to manufacture cotton cloth by the Honduran government. Ironically, because there were no banks in Tegucigalpa, he was forced to keep the money in his own hands.

Due to the efforts of Tennessee governor Peter Turney and the U.S. secretary of state, Ward was arrested and placed in a Tegucigalpa jail. He was arrested in the company of his wife, who refused to leave and remained in Honduras until her husband's fate there could be settled. The opinion was expressed that since his effects, which were considered "princely," had been sequestered, Ward could not bribe his way out of the prison. While it was popularly expected that the forger would soon be sent back to Memphis, there was an impediment. The United States had no treaty of extradition with Honduras, and while the authorities there conceded to the request to have him arrested, they would not extradite until the proper paperwork had been filled out and filed. It was also necessary for the State of Tennessee to send a bona fide witness to Tegucigalpa to make a formal complaint. These matters would take about sixty days to resolve. Thus, Ward remained ensconced in prison, awaiting a special extradition made at the behest of the State Department.[210] Continued difficulties with the State Department sending the official papers led the Honduran government to question why Ward's extradition was delayed. The day after Ward was arrested, a message was received through Minister Young in Guatemala from the State Department that the papers would be sent by an accredited officer on the next steamer, but when the vessel arrived at Puerto Cortez, there was no American agent on board. If the necessary papers were not received shortly, said a spokesman for the Honduran government, Ward would be set free.[211] Ward was released from jail, and he looked about for opportunities to begin a business in Honduras.[212]

While matters simmered, Mrs. Ward left Tegucigalpa for Memphis. Her journey to New Orleans was eventful, as the vessel broke its propeller shaft mid-trip, making her arrival overdue. A horde of newspaper reporters crowded around her as she was hurriedly escorted off the ship by her attorney, sister and parents. She was "heavily wrapped and veiled and did not look up as she passed from the ship to the carriage." She made no comment to the press.[213] (She would later sue for divorce on the grounds of abandonment while Ward was in Honduras.)[214]

Ward was released from the Honduran jail, as the authorities had not received the proper diplomatic papers from Washington, D.C. While free from incarceration, he explored other business opportunities in Central America, all the while remaining anonymous with a "very successful disguise" to avoid arrest. His masquerade consisted of a "pair of blue jeans, overalls, a blue native coat, shaving off his moustache, tying a pebble over his left eye with a big handkerchief and pulling as large straw hat over his face.… [He] would not have been recognized by a Memphis bank teller."

Ward was captured by the Memphis chief of police aboard the ship *City of Dallas* as it carried him incognito to other ports in Central America. He was returned to Memphis, where he claimed he left the city due to his deep sense of shame at having defrauded his victims. His father-in-law agreed to make good some $19,000 worth of Ward's worthless obligations after the forger made bail, but it was not enough to end the controversy. After a lengthy defense against eighty-nine indictments for fraud and malfeasance, the trial was completed in 1900. Ward was found guilty and was sentenced to three years in prison. Perhaps recognizing the seriousness of his transgressions, he volunteered to do his repentance at the infamous Brushy Mountain State Penitentiary, where he arrived on June 20, 1900. Nevertheless, he was released after two and a half years, six months being shaved off his prison term for good behavior. He did not work in the coal mines but in the penitentiary box factory and commissary. His "rich and influential relatives" were an important factor in his early discharge in December 1902.[215] Thereafter, he apparently led an exemplary life, most likely settling in Nashville with his stepfather, Judge E.H. East.[216] Little is known about his life after his release from imprisonment was announced. Most likely, he led a quiet and exemplary life.

# THE BARONESS AND THE LIEUTENANT

## *Love and Espionage in Wartime Chattanooga, 1917–1918*

Chattanooga was as patriotic as any city in the United States during World War I. People were making substantial sacrifices, in President Woodrow Wilson's words, "to make the world safe for democracy." In addition to sacrificing their fortunes and sons, Americans were alert to the possible presence of spies who might sabotage America's war effort. The United States Congress passed the Espionage Act on June 15, 1917. The law provided stiff penalties for those found guilty of aiding the German enemy. It also helped feed public suspicion and rancor toward Germany and all things German.

Anti-German feelings were strong in Tennessee. For example, on December 19, 1917, in Chattanooga, the famous evangelist Billy Sunday told a standing-room-only audience his feelings about the outcome of the war: "I know how it will end. I know that God is on our side. He is not on the side of the Germans or any other fiendish race who will perpetrate such crimes as the Germans have on the women of France and Belgium." At this point, a member of the audience, Mr. Beuterbaugh, walked swiftly to the stage and attacked Sunday. The two grappled momentarily, and Beuterbaugh soon had his hands around Sunday's throat. Sunday pushed his attacker against the piano, and the "crowd swarmed in on Beuterbaugh." Two others "said to be allies of the Hun" began "a little rough house, one of them striking Mayor Asa Candler." There were cries of "Lynch him!" from all sections of the auditorium, but the police arrived to arrest the three who were said to be to be German provocateurs. Several hundred people followed the patrol wagon, threatening violence.[217] In mid-January 1918, it was reported in the *Chattanooga News* that "Dr. Kunwald, director of the Cincinnati Symphony orchestra and a musician of prominence, has been taken into custody by military authorities and interned as a suspicious German in the prison barracks at Fort Oglethorpe. Kunwald was interned once before but released on parole. Actions regarded as suspicious caused his rearrest."[218] In May 1918 in Knoxville, the city school board unanimously voted to remove the study of German language and culture from the public high school curriculum. In August 1918 in Nashville, the *Tennessean* ran an editorial proclaiming that the "alliance between the brewers' organization and German-American disloyalty has been the closest, and the interests of the one are the interests of the other. The brewers of this country are almost entirely German or of German parentage." Tennessee patriotism was fiercely impulsive and anti-German during the war.

It was against this backdrop of anti-German patriotism that an espionage prosecution developed in Chattanooga. While the case was considered momentous, it had many comical, almost farcical facets. The provocative and seductive story of the baroness and the lieutenant was played out in Chattanooga and Knoxville in the winter of 1917–18.

Fort Oglethorpe, just south of Chattanooga in Georgia, was a major induction and training center for the U.S. Army. It was therefore of some major importance to the war effort. Any indisputable or imagined effort to disturb the movement of "Sammies" or "Doughboys" to fight the kaiser would most definitely be considered an act of espionage.

On December 5, 1917, nine months after the United States entered the conflict, the baroness Lona Shope Wilhelmina Sutton Zollner of New York City, the wife of a captain in the German army, stopped in Chattanooga. She was ostensibly on a train trip to Florida. She registered at the Hotel Patten.[219]

Apparently not caring that many in America held a strong anti-German bias, the baroness signed the register as Baroness Lona Zollner and signed all her café checks and cashier slips the same way. She made no attempt to conceal her Teutonic ties. Without a doubt, the baroness attracted attention. As the *Chattanooga Daily News* put it: "Eyes were turned in her direction whenever she passed through the lobby or sat on the mezzanine [of the Hotel Patten.]"[220] Indeed, she seemed determined to be noticed. Shortly after the baroness arrived in Chattanooga, the young Lieutenant J.W.

Spalding, stationed at Fort Oglethorpe as a member of the Sixth United States Infantry, checked into the hotel and became "a frequent visitor in the city." Their love affair did not go unnoticed by the local constabulary or the U.S. Marshal's Office.

Convinced that the two were at least guilty of breaking the city's morality ordinances, the police acted. Shortly after midnight on December 13, both the baroness and Lieutenant J.W. Spalding were arrested—in her hotel room at the Hotel Patten. According to various accounts, she was at first thought to be a lady of the evening, using the hotel room as a place of assignation with the lieutenant. The two were plainly engaged in an infatuated liaison. She was "partly disrobed" at the time of her arrest, while her paramour, Spalding, was discovered "hidden under her bed and only partially clad." The baroness, at the time, claimed the lieutenant was her brother. The couple was taken to Judge O.G. Stone at police headquarters and charged with indecent and immoral behavior and released on bond.[221] However, there was more than a scintillating love affair in the offing.

After her release, the baroness moved to the Park Hotel, where she and Lieutenant Spalding continued their tryst. Spalding had harsh words with the two marshals who followed their movements. The baroness's room was searched for incriminating evidence. Enough existed in the view of the federal agents to place her in the Hamilton County Jail on December 15. Bond was denied. She was charged with being a dangerous alien who had visited near Fort Oglethorpe for an undisclosed but nevertheless "dangerous purpose." United States district attorney W.T. Kennerly, based in Knoxville, had been advised of the goings and comings of the baroness by United States marshal J.R. Thompson. She was to be held until December 22, when she was to be interrogated at a hearing presided over by United States commissioner S.J. McAlester. According to the *Chattanooga Sunday Times*, Kennerly had learned that the baroness "has frequently visited the camp at [Fort] Oglethorpe, has danced with the officers and probably has more than one under her spell….Other activities…establish proof that she is a dangerous person, which [will be] reveal[ed] at the hearing."

The baroness was described as "a striking personage, not so attractive facially, but of winning manner and voluptuous figure. She is vivacious, a characteristic that evidenced itself even while under the fire of the examination by Deputy McMahon." Surmising from "the appearance and talent of the woman while under the fire of cross examination, she would be able to charm secrets out of army officers or others she might get under her spell." Government officials were quoted as saying, "If this woman has not yet succeeded in wringing information of value from young officers [it is because]…they know nothing or because she does not want to learn them."

While in jail, she granted an interview to a *Daily Times* reporter. She was warmed from the chilly temperature of her jail cell by a handsome set of furs drawn tightly over her shoulders. "Between intermittent sobs she talked freely of the charges against her, hysterically denying any relations with the German government." According to the careworn and fatigued baroness:

> *My God, the ignominy of this affair.…To think I have done everything for my country, and not anything against it. I have even fought for the United States, and now I am being held here a prisoner, among poor devils who cry and moan, no doubt to keep up their spirits. This thing will kill me if it injures my dear boy* [at Annapolis], *for I have nothing to fear myself.*

She characterized Lieutenant Spalding as "a dear sweet boy."[222] When she was arrested at the Park Hotel, she claimed Spalding was her husband.[223] According to the reporter, her personal effects were gathered in the cell in two suitcases, which revealed many articles of feminine finery. "On a bench was a package of cigarettes and the prisoner smoked as she talked. 'I learned to smoke while in the old country. Society women smoke and we think nothing of indulging in New York. Smoking is very soothing.'"

"Her interest in Lieut. Spalding was clearly shown, and she did not attempt to conceal the fact that she cares for the young soldier.…As an evidence of her interest in the lieutenant, she stated that he was a dear, sweet boy, and to safeguard him she gave him a letter in which she asked of the Germans should he fall into their hands, that they at least be kind to him." During the interview, the lieutenant tried to call her on the telephone, but he was not allowed to speak with her. News of Spalding's call pleased her greatly.

"'Don't you think it is very cruel?' she asked the reporter, 'To keep me in this dreadful place? My God, boy, do you think if I was guilty of an incriminating act that I would have come to this city and registered in the name of Baroness Zollner?'" She continued: "The incident at the Hotel Patten is very humiliating to me. I solemnly swear to you that I am not guilty of any indiscretion. I have fought for my country, I mean by this that I am responsible for Lieut. Spalding receiving his commission. He was in the training school with my son at Annapolis, and I helped him to pass his examination by urging him to study hard and my mapping out his studies so he could absorb the topics easily." She admitted that her coming to Chattanooga was "very foolish."

According to the newspaper story, the baroness had nothing against the German people, but she did feel sorry for them. Prussian militarism was detestable. "It is true," she said, "that my husband from whom I am attempting to get a divorce, is an officer in the German army." When Bedford Zollner, her youngest son, wrote Baron Zollner with the news he was going to fight for the United States, the German replied: "I am proud of you, my son. Your country first above everything else." The baroness was also concerned that her son, who was on his way to Chattanooga, would be arrested for bringing with him the two quarts of medicinal whiskey she asked him to bring her from New York. "Before coming to Tennessee I did not know that a 'bone dry' law made the bringing of whisky into the state a criminal offense," she said. "We have our wine at home and whisky has been prescribed for me by my physician." At the end of the interview, she "reached for a magazine, and a roach ran from under the cover. 'Oh, these horrible bugs,' she exclaimed. 'And to think I must sleep here tonight. This will be impossible.'"

While investigating the baroness, the police learned that she was born in the United States, was apparently supplied with an abundance of money and one of her deceased husbands was a Bavarian baron, hence her title. She had lived in England for a number of years. She insisted that the lieutenant was just a close family friend and admitted her "partly disrobed" appearance when the detective entered her room. Lieutenant Spalding had only come into her room to get an aspirin tablet, she claimed. "There was nothing unusual about the Lieutenant being in my room," the baroness asserted. Nevertheless, she did admit that he had proposed marriage to her and had come to her room not for a headache cure but to discuss matters matrimonial. They quarreled, and she "took a spell with her heart and fell asleep, to be awakened by the house detective. Spalding was under the bed, and he had his clothes with him." She explained that he hid under the bed because "he would compromise her if found there at that hour of the night—it was about 2 [sic] in the morning." Even with such admissions, the baroness "stated that at no time had her conduct been other than that of a lady."

The baroness lived in the restricted zone in Washington, D.C., an area set aside by the U.S. government for enemy aliens. Residents of the zone were kept under constant surveillance by the Secret Service. Government agents were certain her photograph would soon be found in a Justice Department file. The baroness also lived in opulent surroundings on Park Avenue in New York City. One letter found in her belongings was from a Knoxville woman married to a dangerous alien who was being held under suspicion and was under constant Secret Service surveillance. Other documents found in her room were apparently in some sort of cipher and seemed to address the sailing times and ports of departure of various ships. According to a newspaper report: "The young officer has been under the spell of the woman, or else in reality [is] a friend in the strangest and most mysterious circumstances [known here] for some years."[224] The baroness and the lieutenant had been the objects of a long-standing and ongoing secret service investigation more than a year before the sensational affair was uncovered in Chattanooga.[225]

As the cold snap ended and temperatures soared into the forties, the baroness retained local attorney C.C. Abernathy to defend her. Abernathy filed for a writ of habeas corpus on December 18 in an effort to win freedom for the baroness until her hearing on December 22. His case appeared justified by the news that the baroness had suffered a nervous breakdown and was under the care of a physician. Since being confined in the Hamilton County Jail, she reportedly had slept in a chair, refusing to sleep on the infested jail cot.

According to Abernathy's petition, the baroness claimed to be a native-born citizen of the United States, and although her husband was an officer in the German army, she was in the process of divorcing him. She had stopped to visit Lieutenant Spalding in Chattanooga while on her way to Florida. She was thoroughly interrogated by two federal marshals on December 14 and put up $500 bail, which was accepted. She was then ordered to her room by the marshal. A guard stood at the door. On morning of December 15, the baroness was arrested and taken before H.R. Caulkins, a Hamilton County justice of the peace, who issued a warrant that charged her with espionage. She demanded a trial but was instead placed in the Hamilton County Jail. The baroness, therefore, was due her freedom, especially since she had put up bail. "She doesn't even know what section of the Espionage Act she's charged with violating."[226]

The baroness's request for a writ of habeas corpus was refused. The day before the preliminary hearing, as she languished in her jail cell, her youngest son, Bedford Zollner, arrived from New York to support his mother. The young Zollner, whose father was an officer in the German Imperial Army, was characterized as "very German." He spoke with a strong foreign accent and carried himself like a military-trained schoolboy. He was said to be but sixteen, although he appeared much older. Young Zollner was taken to the jail to visit his mother for several hours. Their reunion "drew emotional sobs and cries from the mother and son, and they held each other in a tight embrace for many minutes." Bedford's request to stay with his mother overnight was refused.

In the meantime, Lieutenant Spalding was under arrest and confined to the limits of the Sixth Infantry Camp at Fort Oglethorpe. He performed his usual duties pending an investigation of his activities. Federal officers were of the opinion that they would want Spalding as a witness at the baroness's hearing. Lieutenant Spalding was to face an inquiry based on the sixty-first article of war, which dealt with personal conduct. "The circumstances of his arrest in Baroness Zollner's room," read an article in the *Chattanooga Daily Press*, "hidden under the bed and only partially clad, as charged by the police, will probably be investigated even though it be determined that he is innocent of intrigue with an alien enemy."[227]

The preliminary hearing was a sensation. The inquest lasted eleven hours, from 10:30 a.m. to 9:30 p.m. Baroness Zollner was called to the stand in a weak condition, and for more than an hour, her voice was barely audible, but as the direct examination proceeded, she grew stronger. When U.S. district attorney Kennerly started his grueling cross-examination, she was firmly in control and did not falter at any time in her testimony.

Kennerly, who in "a manner uncanny at some times" presented facts pertaining to the baroness's matrimonial difficulties, complications and tragedies in her life. Kennerly charged that she was an enemy alien because of her two marriages to German army officers, von Kolberg, whom she divorced because of his "disgrace because of his degeneracy," and Captain Zollner. She was introduced to the German General Staff as a consequence of her marriage to von Kolberg. Worse than that, she had been presented to the kaiser and the empress in Berlin. Kennerly also showed that she had made the acquaintances of prominent army officials in the German and American armies, as well as U.S. congressmen and officials of the Bureau of Inspection. It did not look good for the baroness.

Kennerly then homed in on her relationship with Lieutenant Spalding. Yes, she admitted, they had spent time together in the same hotel in Washington, D.C., on a number of occasions, and she paid the bills for both of them.

> *She admitted without hesitation, her infatuation for Lieut. Spalding, and stated that he was infatuated with her. She admitted having a code, given to her by Spalding, which…*[read in part]*:*

> *Leave soon for Europe via New York City. Everyone well.*

*For Europe via Norfolk. Everybody well.*
*For Europe soon but don't know via which port. All well.*
*In each case if I want to see you I'll say lovingly.*

This, she explained, was a code given to her before Spalding left for Fort Leavenworth for officer training and that he intended to see her before he was sent to France. He also asked her to marry him.

Further evidence revolved around curious notes in Spalding's hand, which "went on in a very rambling and mystifying way about a house in Annapolis." The baroness explained that this was written because of her taking over the Howard house in Annapolis, which, at the time, required her to clean it at her own expense, even though she had rented the house furnished.

The experiences of the baroness, her numerous travels, her various husbands, her numerous divorces and her long association with high army officials in Germany, England and the United States were outlined in great detail. In the cross-examination, it was brought out that the baroness's life had known tragedy. While she stated her German husbands were brutal to her, she also asserted that she had communicated with her estranged husband, Captain Zollner, although she was then suing for divorce.

Adding to the intrigue of her story was testimony concerning her visits to Monte Carlo, Nice and Jahore (the "Monte Carlo of the East") and her ownership of a rubber plantation near Singapore. Light was shed on her influence with British major general Sir Alfred Turner. Through her clout, she convinced Turner to release Captain Zollner from a concentration camp in England for enemy aliens after war had been declared, and the captain subsequently and suddenly disappeared from England and arrived in America with a fraudulent passport. Zollner then returned to Germany to fight for the kaiser—after he had given his word of honor not to take up arms against England. This was stressed and admitted to by the baroness. She also admitted to having come to the United States some years ago with Baron Von Loevenfeldt as the guest of Andrew Carnegie. Her function was to give advice about what kind of speeches Von Loevenfeldt should make during his goodwill tour in America aimed at generating a better feeling for Germany.

Her relations with Lieutenant Spalding, already the object of public probing, were amplified. The baroness testified that she assisted Spalding pass his examination for a commission in the United States Army after meeting him about a year before in Annapolis, Maryland. She also testified to having advanced Spalding money for a railroad ticket to officer candidate school in Fort Leavenworth, Kansas. Yes, she met Spalding on a number of occasions in Washington, D.C., where she had gone to see Congressman George William Loft of New York to ensure her son's appointment to the United States Naval Academy. Neither did the beleaguered baroness deny going to Washington and stopping at the Congress Hall after Spalding's commission was granted, meeting him there on several occasions.

Her relations with Spalding at the Patten Hotel were the subject of a mild sensation in the long trial. She said that when the lieutenant was caught in her room, he was disrobed and she was partly dressed. She stated that he had come there to talk over some matters pertaining to their upcoming marriage and that they had quarreled. He again came to her room and stated that he was going to stay all night. The baroness said "that she took a spell with her heart, and fell asleep, to be awakened by the house detective. Spalding was under the bed and had his clothes with him. She denied having been indiscreet with Spalding, and stated that at no time had her conduct been other than that of a lady."[228]

*United States District Attorney honed in on her recent liaisons with the lieutenant:*

*Do you mean to say that you have had no immoral relations with Spalding?*

*I have not.*

*He was found in your room wasn't he?*

*He was.*

*He was disrobed, was he not? And you were only partly dressed. How do you explain that?*

*I had quarreled with Mr. Spalding and he returned to my room when I was in the act of retiring. He stated that he was going to stay all night. I told him he had better not. I was stricken with one of my spells, and laid down dressed as I was. I was awakened by a knock on the door. Lieutenant Spalding was still in the room.*

*You stated that you knew nothing of Mr. Spalding undressing?*

*No.*

*You knew he intended staying all night?*

*Yes.*

*You didn't put him out, did you?*

*No.*

*You say you have no recollection of what he had on, but you remember that you both dressed so you could be taken to police headquarters?*

*Yes.*

*He spoke to you in endearing tones, did he not, saying: "When are you going*
*to get your divorce, dearie?"*
*I do not remember.*[229]

Taking up her defense, attorney C.C. Abernathy concentrated on the tactics and actions of Marshals Thompson and McMahon. He grilled the federal officers severely, especially McMahon. Abernathy's interrogation included the following scolding:

*You were pretty excited when you made the arrest of Mrs. Zollner weren't*
*you Mr. McMahon?…You wouldn't stand the same rough treatment you*
*accorded Mrs. Zollner, would you, Mr. McMahon? You made a threat that*
*if she did tell you what you wanted to know she would stay in jail all her*
*life and Mr. Spalding would be shot the following Sunday morning. When*
*she mentioned her children, you shook your finger in her face and said: "You*
*ain't got no children," didn't you?*[230]

The only mention of the words *German spy* and the incident that brought the only gasp from the spectators manifested when a telegram from federal operatives in Boston to attorney Ed Finley of the Department of Justice was read. It stipulated that the baroness's sister-in-law had been questioned by federal agents. The telegram continued that she stated that her husband said he knew his sister, the baroness, was active in this country as a German spy and that he himself had furnished information to her from a cantonment in Massachusetts.

After being confronted with the evidence in the telegram, the baroness stated that her brother, Adrian, had brought disgrace on her family in New York due to his alcoholism. She had refused to continue funding his dependency after he reached rock bottom and likewise refused to aid his former wife, whom he divorced because of her own impecunious condition. Her sister-in-law, explained the baroness, was motivated by revenge.

The prosecution endeavored then to show that the baroness's friendship with naval, military and government officials was for the purpose of furthering her alleged "activities as a servant of the German government." The defense countered that the baroness, because she was categorized as a dangerous enemy alien and under secret service surveillance, was compelled to advise the naval intelligence department of her presence in Chattanooga, which she did. But the prosecution established the fact that she had not been given permission to visit Fort Oglethorpe. She admitted having gone to the fort twice. This constituted the only tangible evidence of her violation of the Espionage Act.

Other testimony included that of Marshal Jack Thompson. He told of the arrest and the discovery of numerous letters and documents, which were turned over to prosecuting attorney Kennerly. Other witnesses included the house detective at the Patten, and William Bryan, the Park hotel detective, related the embarrassing arrest of the baroness on December 13 by Marshall Thompson and Deputy McMahon.

Julian B. Shope, the New York lawyer and brother of Charles Warren Shope, Baroness Zollner's first husband, testified to her good character, categorically stating that he had never heard the defendant express any sentiment for or against Germany.

Finally, United States deputy McMahon was put on the stand and furnished the humor of the day. The baroness's attorney, C.C. Abernathy, chastised the deputy for his brusque manner of quizzing the baroness at different times. Deputy McMahon, claimed the defense attorney, used bombastic tactics and disturbed her "mental condition to such an extent that she had prayed she would never have to see him again." Due to the lateness of the hour, both Bedford Zollner and Lieutenant Spalding were scheduled to testify at the next session on Christmas Eve. The hearing was attended by a large crowd of spectators, many of whom were men in officers' uniforms.[231]

At the end of the proceedings, the baroness was taken back to her cell and allowed no visitors, save her son, who was accompanied by Ed Finley, an attorney with the Department of Justice. Bedford Zollner, the baroness and Lieutenant Spalding were scheduled to take the witness stand when the inquiry continued on Christmas Eve.[232]

In court the next day, Kennerly introduced new evidence in the form of letters that were sent between Bedford Zollner and his mother. One "letter described the rough roads to and from Fort Oglethorpe, the 'abysmal topography' of the land contiguous to the cantonment, and their 'rough huts' erected for the soldiers with their small iron bed furnishings." This constituted probable cause and was regarded as tangible evidence against the defendant and used to establish her guilt under section 2 of the Espionage Act. After presenting his evidence, Kennerly called the baroness "the most consummate actress I have ever seen on the witness stand."

Other information gleaned from the trial was hardly germane to the issue at hand, but it was sensational. Attorney Abernathy attributed the baroness's transgressions to Lieutenant Spalding's being a "fool boy" who was madly infatuated with her. He justified their relations with the old expression "love is blind." Even though she was forty-four and he twenty-two, no one could say that they did not love each other. Nonetheless, it was Spalding who was responsible for the woman's humiliation, for the complex situations in which she found herself since stopping in Chattanooga only twenty days earlier. The defense council concluded, telling the court that the baroness had a little daughter, Nonie, back in New York who was looking for her mother. Abernathy was overcome with pity, and it was reported that "this last statement affected the attorney for he stopped off short and tears appeared in the eyes of the defendant."

Finally composed, the defense attorney showed how it was that, at Annapolis, she first was considered a German spy. While at a tea party there before the American entry into the war, she defended Germany and excused the sinking of the *Lusitania*. The twists and permutations of her life were astonishing. Born an eccentric millionaire's daughter in New York City, she owned a rubber plantation near Singapore, was a world traveler, had married five times, had won the trust of high-level officials in Germany, England and America and was related to the Roosevelt family by marriage. She was at least neutral in her attitude toward the war because, in 1916, the baroness gave "an entertainment in New York… for the benefit the orphans of French soldiers."[233] She vigorously denied the charges of espionage. According to the *New York Times*, "She said she had been investigated at Washington and Annapolis, and was permitted to move about under the known status of an enemy alien."[234]

Lieutenant Spalding was the next witness on the stand. He testified candidly that, yes, notwithstanding the twenty-two-year gap in their ages, he loved the baroness and believed she loved him, too. He acknowledged that he had given her a code to enable her to keep up with his movements should he ship out. He wanted to marry her. "He confessed to having urged her to come to Chattanooga to be beside him because he was 'proud' to have others see her with him."

During Kennerly's cross-examination of Spalding, it was learned that the baroness was prone to having "melancholy spells," in which she attempted to take her life. Spalding testified that he always had been afraid that the baroness would carry out her numerous threats to harm herself. Kennerly continued:

> *You contemplated marrying the baroness to get possession of her rubber estate, didn't you?*
> *I did, sir. I was going to be her manager. She offered me the position.*

*When the house detective knocked on the baroness' door at the Hotel Patten,
    where were you?*
*I don't know. Under the bed, I think.*
*Were you on the bed beforehand?*
*I was, sir. Reclining there.*
*Who got off the bed first? You or the baroness?*
*I did, sir.*
*What did you do?*
*I tried to find a place to hide, sir.*

The courtroom resounded in laughter at this last response.

Bedford Zollner, the baroness's son, was remarkable. His performance "brought surprise and recognition from the court and the audience. His testimony could not be shaken." He seemed to know as much about his mother's history as the baroness herself. He also was familiar with Spalding and his movements around Annapolis. He stated that he was more responsible for his mother coming to this city any anyone else. He informed Commissioner McAllester that he urged her to go to Chattanooga for a restful visit. He had never heard his mother say anything against the United States government or make any utterances favorable to Germany. He frankly substantiated his mother's charge of the cruelty of Captain Zollner. After the court recessed, Bedford's mother was sequestered without bail in the Hamilton County jail on Christmas Eve 1917.[235]

There she remained incarcerated, and on New Year's Day, Judge E.T. Sanford of the United States District Court granted a hearing for the writ of habeas corpus in the espionage case to be heard within twenty days. In the meantime, the baroness lingered in jail.[236] The *Knoxville Journal and Tribune* was prompted to comment that she "is a woman of culture and it is said that the confinement in the jail at Chattanooga…is telling on her nerves and appearance." The populace in Knoxville was beginning to take more notice of the case, especially since the trial was to be transferred to that city for hearing. "It is expected the federal court house there would be crowded to overflowing once the hearing was to begin."[237] Soon came news that the baroness's divorce was thrown out of court in Maryland because neither she nor Captain Zollner appeared for a hearing. She, of course, was in jail, and he was an officer in the enemy's army.

Baroness Zollner, it was reported, had been suffering a great deal with a sore throat. Dr. J. McChesney Hogshead had been attending the noted prisoner. Late in the afternoon on Monday, January 7, it was announced that the baroness was in a very serious condition. Nevertheless, the spunky baroness still expressed her confidence that she would be acquitted upon the hearing before Judge E.T. Sanford at Knoxville.[238]

By January 9, Judge E.T. Sanford set the date for a hearing on a writ of habeas corpus for January 16 in Knoxville. According to one report, the baroness's health was rapidly declining, and the government appointed physician recommended that she be allowed immediately to leave the jail cell "or the result will be fatal." Attorney C.C. Abernathy claimed on that basis, "her physical and mental condition has been greatly impaired since her commitment to jail, and that her physical and mental condition is growing worse daily, on account of her confinement." Compounding these developments was the news that the baroness was suffering from an acute attack of laryngitis "of such a virulent nature that she has been forced to call a specialist.…Confinement in jail has almost exhausted… [her]…physical strength, and she avers and believes that further confinement will be fatal to her." Her three children, one a midshipman in Annapolis, Beresford Shope; Bedford Zollner; and a six-and-a-half-year-old girl in New York, were all the objects of severe stress resulting from the proceedings.[239] In the meantime, Marshal Thompson had inspected the prison facilities in Knoxville and found them in excellent condition. One report had it that the "authorities are anxious that, while she is kept in strict confinement at all times, she shall have no reason to complain about the condition of her quarters."[240]

The effect of the long confinement in the Hamilton County Jail was perceptible on the Baroness Lona W. Zollner as she walked down the jail steps to begin her passage to Knoxville, where her next hearing was scheduled before Judge E.T. Sanford. She was guarded by Hamilton County sheriff Nick P. Bush and U.S. marshal J.R. Thompson. She was careworn and gaunt. "She stated that her imprisonment," the *Chattanooga News* reported, "on account of its absolute injustice had seriously impaired her health and from an apparently strong vivacious woman she has changed to a thin and weak one." The beleaguered and besieged baroness was incapable of speaking above a whisper because of her acute laryngitis. She had been given a thorough physical examination the day before. The results were thought to support her plea for a writ of habeas corpus. Her attorney was confident that he had his case well prepared and "would be able to spring some surprises at the trial."[241]

The baroness arrived in Knoxville and was escorted to the Knox County Jail, not being permitted to spend the night in a hotel. While incarcerated, she conversed with newspaper reporters and smoked cigarettes "to steady her nerves." She was very courteous to visitors and most congenial in her speech. C.C. Abernathy proclaimed her innocence on the charge of espionage, even though she "more or less indiscreetly carried on." Her detention in jail was, claimed the baroness, the cause of her recent nervous breakdown. Should she be granted a writ of habeas corpus, the baroness said, she would return to Chattanooga and stay in a sanitarium or hospital until she might recuperate from her present trouble. The baroness excused herself from further interviews, saying she was too nervous and tired to talk. "She said she felt badly unnerved and requested…a nurse or some good companion with whom she could talk and who would cheer her in her depression." Both of her sons were in Knoxville to testify and otherwise support their mother in her hour of need. It was leaked to the press that that Deputy District Attorney William Kennerly would introduce new evidence that would question the 100 percent Americanism of the baroness's sons, especially Beresford.[242]

Many Knoxville residents, especially women, were interested in if not hostile toward the baroness. For example, the police were called out to disperse a crowd of more than two hundred persons who "congregated [that night]…outside of a restaurant in which the baroness was eating."[243] Future incidents involving hostile women would accent the trial. It was the presence of hostile Knoxville women that resulted in the court being cleared of all but police, witnesses and members of the press.

On January 15, the courtroom was cleared of hundreds of women who, like Madame La Farge, had "gathered and had brought their knitting." In the corridor outside the courtroom, a young woman with the moniker "just plain Billie" was assaulted. It seems "just plain Billie" (or "Billie from Phillie") loudly asserted the reality of the situation, namely that "the public was doing the baroness and injustice by presuming that the woman was guilty before she was tried." In the crowd of women surging from the room, a forty-five-year-old "refined looking lady swung a hard left straight to the right eye" with a "gloved fist," giving "just plain Billie" a "K-O blow." As a report in the *Chattanooga News* put it: "The sentiment against the prisoner is much stronger here than in Chattanooga, some of the remarks of the women reaching a vicious state."[244] It was later divulged that "Billie" was a former private investigator in New York City and was now a government secret agent.[245]

During the trial, it was revealed that the government authorities had in their possession a letter that was written by Beresford Zollner on the night of his graduation from preparatory school. In it, he stated that he had gone down to visit an old German in Annapolis who ran a German museum. From the elderly man, he learned how to sing the German national anthem "Deuthchland [*sic*] Uber Alles." Even more damning was the statement that he was very proud to have learned to sing "the Prussian battle song." Still more profane, it was reported "[f]rom the early hours of night until the wee small hours of morning did young Zollner sing 'Deutchland Uber Alles.'"

Other new pieces of evidence included the tale that once while at lunch at Annapolis, the baroness made a remark that one local grande dame took as an insult to the United States. In retaliation, she "threw a cup of tea into the face of Mrs. Zollner, and later on shrieked out at her 'German spy!'" Also testifying on the Americanism of Beresford Zollner were Lieutenant Commander Fowler of Naval Intelligence and Captain Everly from the U.S. Naval Academy.[246]

A few minutes after 9:00 a.m. on January 16, Baroness Zollner took her seat at the habeas corpus hearing. While Baroness Zollner appeared well composed when she entered the courtroom, her hand twitched restively as she took the oath. District Attorney W.T. Kennerly asked Judge Sanford to clear the nearly standing-room-only courtroom of all spectators and witnesses, including the baroness's two sons. The crowd of spectators, mostly women, were unhappy. According to the *Knoxville Journal and Tribune*:

> *The large number of society women seemed especially disappointed at not being allowed to remain and hear the evidence, and many of them waited outside the doors for hours hoping to get another glimpse at the baroness, whose…auburn hair seemed to be the center of attraction.*

There followed the by now hackneyed reiteration of her arrest in the hotel room with the lieutenant. Under questioning by Marshal Thompson, she admitted her German descent and said that her father was a native of Germany. She admitted having been in touch with, through a third party, Captain Zollner at least fifteen times since he rejoined the German army in 1914. And she said she had received at least thirty-six letters from her German husband since that time. Nevertheless, she proclaimed her complete loyalty to President Wilson and stoutly maintained that she was innocent of any violation of the Espionage Act. The court recessed until 2:30.[247]

But the court did not resume at 2:30, because the baroness was released at 4:00 in a surprise ruling. Her bond was set at $2,500 after Kennerly and

Abernathy reached a deal. The bond was signed for by Abernathy. Judge Sanford also ruled that the personal letters introduced as evidence were immaterial to the bail-bond cases. According to the judge:

> *These letters and all of this matter you are going into is a waste of time Mr. Kennerly. They don't help me. The more you produce the more you show me of the woman's infatuation for Spalding. You are strengthening her case and not helping me a bit. I have already made up my mind that the defendant was infatuated with Spalding and I don't care to hear any other evidence, unless you can show that through her intimacy she has gained information to help the German government. This does not mean that the evidence you have is incompetent when produced at the trial, but as this is a question of bail, I must rule that it has no bearing on the case.*[248]

There were conditions placed on the release of Mrs. Zollner, namely that she refrain from communicating with persons in the military or naval services of the United States, as well as all persons in Austria and Germany for the duration of the war. The only exception was her son at the Naval Academy. The Baroness Zollner and her two sons left soon thereafter for Chattanooga. It was also announced that the baroness would not be allowed to sue Captain Zollner for divorce until after the war. She must live at her New York Park Avenue address and not "go near the docks there, while she is to notify District Attorney Kennerly of her whereabouts and actions twice each week." She was not excused from her espionage trial, which was to be held in Chattanooga.[249]

Once back in Chattanooga, the Baroness Wilhelmina W. Sutton Zollner was "radiantly happy, and very exuberant" over the result of her bond hearing. She was finding it very difficult to adjust herself again to normal surroundings. According to one newspaper report, even though "snow fell and the sun shone but little, hers was a day in May. Gone were the signs of the imprisoned woman, overshadowed by the accusation of German spy.… Youthfulness and buoyancy chased away the aging imp of care, and charm returned to assert itself in happy expressions, in engaging conversation."

The baroness wore her finest jewelry and festively spoke to reporters in her room at the Park Hotel. She clearly said that it was hard not to look for iron bars and adjust herself to a less restrictive environment. The baroness, nevertheless, was not bitter and harbored no acrimony. In summation, the still-indicted baroness said, "I cannot express my gratitude nor my appreciation of the splendid treatment I have received both in this city and

Knoxville. I shall go away and shall never forget those who have been good to me, kind to me."[250]

She harbored no malice and broke "into smiles when she told her Chattanooga friends good-bye on Monday the 21st of January. According to the baroness, 'I can never tell how kind the people here at the Park hotel have been to me. Every day that I was in the jail they sent me linen and food and kept me comfortable. And then there was 'Dopey' [the jail custodian] who came to seem Sunday and said that the jail felt lonesome without me. I was real amused at him." Her sense of humor, which was never subdued during her ordeal, played over her experience in Chattanooga, and she was inclined to think of it lightly. She said that she could not refrain from laughing when she looked back on some of the things that had happened.[251]

Meanwhile, District Attorney Kennerly insisted that the baroness's case would be tried during the April term of the court. Many, however, doubted that the trial would ever take place and "the conditions of the bond were made merely to save [Kennerly] in case the that it was never brought up. Whether the baroness is guilty the public will never know. Some of her actions were unexplainable, but in all she gave a plausible account of her actions. The government attorneys have not been able to gather...a strong case against her and will be forced to rely upon circumstances. At any rate she has left Chattanooga and the odds are against her coming back in April for trial."[252]

Baroness Zollner never did stand trial. W.T. Kennerly was faced with a peculiar case. The facts of the case were not enough to call for a conviction, and for that reason, the circumstances had to be relied on entirely. "Judge Sanford all through the hearing...discouraged the district attorney to such an extent that it is barely possible that he will attempt to bake the case further. While the hearing was yet in progress he arranged with the baroness's attorney for bond, and the opinion of the court was that the 'prisoner be allowed to as agreed by the attorneys.' The hearing was never finished and was not put up to the judge for his decision." There's no doubt that her relationship to the Roosevelt family had a greater bearing on the case than the press was made aware of at the time.[253]

While the baroness enjoyed her freedom at her swanky 780 Madison Avenue address, her son Beresford Shope was forced to resign from the Naval Academy, according to the *New York Times*, "on account of letters written to his mother...showing he was in sympathy with pro-German views." Baroness Zollner remained under close federal surveillance and was bound to live up to the conditions of her bond.[254] The fate of the Lieutenant

J.W. Spalding of the Sixth U.S. Infantry is not known, nor, for the matter, is that of the baroness after the war in Europe ended.

If the baroness was a spy, she was hardly a Mata Hari. The young lieutenant could scarcely be considered a fountainhead of military secrets the German enemy might covet. Perhaps the two were in love, but it was a love destined to unravel in the intense anti-German climate of America. Information on the fate of the baroness and the lieutenant in the postwar world is sketchy at best, but if there were further intimacies, it is doubtful they took place in Chattanooga.

# NOTES

*Chapter 1*

1. *Memphis Daily Appeal*, October 30, 1860; November 2, 1860; November 3, 1860; November 13, 1860; November 14, 1860. See also: *Semi-weekly Mississippian*, November 16, 1860; *Daily Mississippian*, November 27, 1860, as cited in Tennessee State Library and Archives, Nineteenth Century. The concept of a committee of public safety was born of the French Revolution, when the committee of public safety was created in 1793 by the National Convention. Established as an administrative body, it transmogrified into an agency to protect the revolution from outside reactionary forces. As it worked to meet these threats, it became more and more powerful and ruled France during the Terror. While there are similarities to the French precedent, the committees in Tennessee were local and only loosely connected with each other.
2. *New York Times*, August 3, 1857.
3. *Memphis Daily Appeal*, October 30, 1860; November 2, 1860; November 3, 1860; November 13, 1860; November 14, 1860. See also: *Semi-weekly Mississippian*, November 16, 1860; *Daily Mississippian*, November 27, 1860, as cited in Tennessee State Library and Archives, Nineteenth Century.
4. *Louisville Journal*, December 17, 1860.
5. William G. Stevenson, *Thirteen Months in the Rebel Army* (New York: A.S. Barnes and Company, 1862), 31–33.
6. *Harper's Weekly Magazine*, March 29, 1862, 202.

7. *Daily Cleveland Herald*, April 20, 1861, as cited in Tennessee State Library and Archives, Nineteenth Century.
8. Part II, in *Official Records of the War of the Rebellion*, vol. 52, Series I, 67. Hereinafter cited as *OR*.
9. *OR*, 154.
10. 1860 federal census, Shelby County, TN (186l), 449, 450, 704, 721, 732, 860, 876, 959, 976; enslaved census data from http://www.ancestor.com.
11. *Nashville Union and American*, April 24, 1861.
12. Broadside Collection, Tennessee State Library and Archives.
13. *Daily Cleveland Herald*, April 25, 1861.
14. Ibid.
15. John Wooldridge, *History of Nashville, Tennessee* (Nashville, TN: C. Elder, 1875), 191–92. Although the organization is not referenced in Nashville newspapers after August 1861, it continued its activities. See also: *Papers of Andrew Johnson*, vol. 5, *1861–1862* (Knoxville: University of Tennessee Press, 1979), 368fn3.
16. *Louisville Journal*, October 28, 1861, as cited from the *New York Times* October 12, 1861, as cited in Pro Quest Civil War.
17. *Milwaukee Daily Sentinel*, March 11, 1861. This notion would be made state law on June 28, 1861. See also: Chapter 24, in eleven sections, passed by the 31st (Confederate) General Assembly, relative to the authorization of the governor to draft free persons of color into the Army of Tennessee, *Public Acts of the State of Tennessee*, passed at the extra session of the 33rd General Assembly, April 1861 (Nashville, TN: J.G. Griffith & Co., Public Printers, Union and American Office, 1861), 49–50. See also: *OR*, vol. 1, Series IV, 409. It is difficult to imagine what they were thinking.
18. *Memphis Daily Appeal*, May 14, 15, 1861.
19. *Philadelphia Inquirer*, May 16, 1861, as cited in Tennessee State Library and Archives, Nineteenth Century.
20. *Louisville Journal*, May 23, 1861; *Bangor Daily Whig Courier*, May 30, 1861, as cited in Tennessee State Library and Archives, Nineteenth Century.
21. *Bangor Daily Whig Courier*, May 14, 1861; May 15, 1861. *Philadelphia Inquirer*, May 16, 1861, as cited in Tennessee State Library and Archives, Nineteenth Century. *Daily Whig & Courier*, May 23, 1861, as cited in Tennessee State Library and Archives, Nineteenth Century.
22. *Louisville Journal*, July 2, 1861.
23. James Whitelaw would later lead a rebel guerrilla band in West Tennessee. See also: *OR*, vol. 5, Series II, 821–22.
24. *Louisville Journal*, May 31, 1861.

25. During the Mexican-American War, Brigadier General Gideon Pillow ordered an earthen fortification to be built at the Mexican town of Camargo. It was constructed so that it faced U.S. forces and not the Mexican army—that is, completely backward. The incident followed Pillow, giving him a warranted reputation for incompetence; *Louisville Journal*, June 4, 1861.

26. *Philadelphia Inquirer*, June 8, 1861, as cited in Tennessee State Library and Archives, Nineteenth Century.

27. *Louisville Journal*, June 3, 1861.

28. *Louisville Journal*, June 5, 1861.

29. Evidence to support this contention has proven elusive.

30. As cited in Frank Moore, ed., *The Rebellion Record: A Diary of American Events, with Documents, Narratives, Illustrative Events, Poetry*, 11 vols. (New York: D. Van Nostrand, Publisher, 1867–68) 2:58.

31. Ibid.

32. Amanda McDowell, Entry for June 9, 1861, in *Diary of Amanda McDowell*, edited by Lela McDowell Blankenship, 2nd ed. (New York: Richard R. Smith, 1943; repr. Utica, KY: McDowell Publications, 1988), 81–82.

33. *Louisville Journal*, July 2, 1861.

34. Charles C. Bolton, *Poor Whites of the Antebellum South: Tenants and Laborers in Central North Carolina and Northeast Mississippi* (Durham, NC: Duke University Press, 2003), 165.

35. *Louisville Daily Journal*, June 13, 1861, as cited in PQCW.

36. *Harper's Weekly Illustrated* 5, no. 234 (June 22, 1861): 394 (illustration), 397 (text).

37. *Liberator*, July 19, 1861, as cited in Tennessee State Library and Archives, Nineteenth Century.

38. Letter not found.

39. The narrator provided the committee of vigilance's arresting officer as "THURMAN."

40. A similar account is found in the *Boston Herald*, August 9, 1861.

41. *Philadelphia Inquirer*, July 22, 1861, as cited in Tennessee State Library and Archives, Nineteenth Century.

42. *Boston Herald*, August 9, 1861, as cited in Tennessee State Library and Archives, Nineteenth Century.

43. This is a likely illustration of Charles Bolton's assertion in *Poor Whites in the Antebellum South* that committees of vigilance focused on "transient poor white men." That is, men with clean shirts were neither poor nor transient.

44. *Frank Leslie's Illustrated Newspaper*, September 14, 1861, as cited in Tennessee State Library and Archives, Nineteenth Century.

45. *Louisville Journal*, August 27, 1861.

46. Judge John Catron was born in Virginia in 1781. After serving with Andrew Jackson in the War of 1812, he was elected to the Tennessee Supreme Court in 1824. President Jackson appointed him to the United States Supreme Court in 1824. Seven years later, he was chosen as the first chief justice of the Supreme Court. Catron was, from the beginning to the end, a strong advocate of the Federal Union, sentiments that caused him trouble in Nashville in 1861. The vigilance committee called on him and advised him to resign from his seat on the Supreme Court or leave Tennessee within twenty-four hours. Catron most likely would not have left Nashville but for the threat to his life and the probability that his wife's health would suffer. After the war, he returned to Nashville, where he died on May 30, 1865. See: History of the Sixth Circuit, http://www.ca6. uscourts.gov/lib_hist/Courts/supreme/judges/jc-bio.html.

47. As cited in the *New York Times*, August 18, 1861.

48. *Louisville Journal*, July 31, 1861, and August 3, 13, 28, 1861; *New York Herald*, August 14, 1862; *Nashville Union and American*, July 31, 1861, as cited in *Louisville Journal*, August 3, 1861; *New York Herald*, August 14, 1861, as cited in PQCW.

49. *OR*, vol. 2, Series II, 1,369–370. See also: Jennete Blakely Frost, *The Rebellion in the United States*, 2 vols. (New York: n.p., 1865), 333.

50. *Philadelphia Inquirer*, August 28, 1861.

51. *OR*, vol. 52, Series I, 134–35.

52. *OR*, vol. 10, Series I, 640–41; *OR*, vol. 1, Series II, 882, 884.

53. A.N. Edmonds, Sam Tate, N.S. Bruce, W.G. Ford, J.M. Patrick, J.M. Gondir, James A. Carnes, F.W. Royster, F. Titus, Q.C. Atkinson, Saml. P. Walker, S.T. Watson, et al., Committee of Public Safety (Memphis, TN); *OR*, vol. 4, Series I, 497–98; *OR*, vol. 4, Series I, 497–98.

54. *OR*, vol. 52, Series I, 230–31.

55. *Memphis Daily Appeal*, April 16, 1862, as cited in PQCW.

56. Robin D.G. Kelley, *Race Rebels: Culture, Politics, and the Black Working Class* (New York: Free Press, 1996), 21–22.

57. *Louisville Daily Journal*, February 26, 1862, as cited in PQCW.

58. *Nashville Daily Union*, April 24, 1862, as cited at http://www.uttyl.edu.vbetts.

59. As cited in the *Louisville Journal*, April 30, 1862, as cited in PQCW.

*Chapter 2*

60. James B. Jones Jr., "Manning the Brakes in Antebellum Memphis and Nashville, Tennessee," *Courier* 23, no. 1 (October 1984): 4–5, 7.

61. *Memphis Daily Enquirer*, May 15, 1849.

62. For examples, see: *Memphis Weekly Appeal*, May 2, 1855. See also: James B. Jones Jr., "The Social Aspects of the Memphis Volunteer Fire Department," *West Tennessee Historical Society Papers*, vol. 37 (1983): 62–73. With the introduction of steam-powered fire engines in the late 1850s, the need for volunteer firemen was greatly diminished, and the appearance of paid municipally controlled fire departments was initiated.

63. James B. Jones Jr., "Mose the Bowery B'hoy and the Nashville Volunteer Fire Department, 1849–1860," *Tennessee Historical Quarterly* 40, no. 2 (Summer 1981): 170–81.

64. *Nashville American*, May 3, 1878; July 5, 1878; March 2, 1881; May 26, 1882; May 11, 1883; May 26, 1883; September 2, 1890; May 20, 1892; May 22, 1895; June 1, 1896; March 3, 1897; September 14, 1897; September 17, 1897; September 22, 1897; September 29, 1897; May 8, 1900; September 28, 1900; February 18, 1904; March 10, 1907; March 12, 1907; September 16, 1910; September 20, 1910; June 3, 1918; *Nashville Tennessean and Nashville American*, June 1, 1896; September 12, 1907; October 11, 1907; June 23, 1911; September 21, 1911; April 14, 1912; September 9, 1912; September 12, 1912; September 2, 1913; February 29, 1916; June 4, 1916; August 7, 1916; September 24, 1917; June 3, 1918; July 5, 1918; June 10, 1919; *Nashville Tennessean*, June 1, 1905; October 11, 1907; June 6, 1909; July 7, 1909. Although the centennial for Tennessee's admittance into the Union was 1896, poor planning caused the official celebration to be put off one year.

65. There was also a sham battle portraying the fight at New Orleans presented as part of the Irish Day Parade held during the Tennessee bicentennial. See also: *Nashville American*, September 17, 1897. Sham battles were common forms of entertainment in the nineteenth century. See also: James B. Jones Jr., "Tennessee Military Drill Teams, ca. 1874–1889," *Courier* 61, no. 1 (February 2013): n.p.

66. Today, it is the Sons of Confederate Veterans, or SCV.

67. *Nashville Tennessean*, June 9, 1909.

68. Ibid.

69. *Nashville American*, May 24, 1909.

70. Ibid.; *Nashville American*, June 9, 1909; *Memphis Commercial Appeal*, June 11, 1909.
71. *Nashville Tennessean*, June 9, 1909.
72. *Nashville American*, June 9, 1909; *Memphis Commercial Appeal*, June 11, 1909.
73. *Memphis Commercial Appeal*, June 11, 1909; *Nashville Tennessean*, June 11, 1909.
74. See: James B. Jones Jr., "'General' John Hugh ('Jehazy') McDowell: A Brief Biography of a Confederate Veteran and Political Maverick (1844–1927)," *Courier* (October 1998): n.p. McDowell issued strict guidelines for the parade, including a ban on automobiles, the position and number of carriages in the procession and an absolute sanction on advertisements on any carriage. See also: Nashville *American*, May 23, 1909.
75. *Memphis Commercial Appeal*, June 11, 1909.
76. Ibid. Press coverage was somewhat ambiguous about whether the young Forrest was Forrest II or Forrest III.
77. *Memphis Commercial Appeal*, June 11, 1909.
78. Ibid., Grant, who was on his way to attend the unveiling of a monument to a dead hero of the "Lost Cause" in Vicksburg, Mississippi, stopped in Memphis on the invitation of the Confederate veterans. He was the major general in command of the Eastern Division of the U.S. Army, which included the Department of the East and the Department of the Gulf.
79. *Memphis Commercial Appeal*, June 11, 1909.
80. *Nashville Tennessean*, June 11, 1909.
81. *Memphis Commercial Appeal*, June 11, 1909; *Nashville Tennessean*, June 11, 1909.
82. *Nashville Tennessean*, June 11, 1909.
83. *Memphis Commercial Appeal*, June 11, 1909.
84. Ibid. Most likely, the footage of the parade has been lost or destroyed.
85. *Nashville Tennessean*, June 11, 1909. See also: *Nashville American*, June 11, 1909.
86. *Memphis Daily Appeal*, April 26, 1861; May 29, 1861.
87. *Memphis Commercial Appeal*, June 11, 1909.
88. *Nashville American*, June 11, 1909.
89. *Memphis Commercial Appeal*, June 11, 1909.
90. Ibid.
91. *Nashville American*, June 11, 1909. The Southern Cross Drill was a lively two-step dance.
92. *Memphis Commercial Appeal*, June 11, 1909.
93. It is worth mentioning that the *Official Journal of the United Confederate Veterans* had very little to say about the events in Memphis. Neither the encounters with General Grant nor the appearance of Nathan Bedford

Forrest III were mentioned. See: *Official Journal of the United Confederate Veterans* 17, no. 1 (July 1909): 314–16.

94. *Nashville Banner*, January 9, 1915; *Nashville Tennessean and American*, January 5, 1915.

95. Ibid. Aside from the cotton bales, historical verisimilitude was not a hallmark of the sham battle. See also: *Nashville Banner*, January 9. 1915.

96. *Nashville Banner, Tennessean and American*, January 9, 1915.

97. Ibid. Her remarks about "free born American citizens" excluded foreign-born immigrants, believed by many of her status to be a threat to American life and culture and their preeminent status in American life.

98. *Nashville Banner, Tennessean and American*, January 9, 1915.

99. Tom Kannon, "Forging the 'Hero of New Orleans': Tennessee Looks at the Centennial of the War of 1812," *Tennessee Historical Quarterly* 71, no. 2. (Summer 2012): 128–61.

## Chapter 3

100. *Nashville Daily American*, January 27, 1888; February 13, 1889; June 26, 1910.

101. *Nashville Daily American*, July 4, 1882.

102. *Nashville Daily American*, August 31, 1875; August 26, 1888. See also: *Nashville Daily American*, July 3, 1916.

103. *Nashville Daily American*, September 17, 1875.

104. *Nashville Daily American*, August 31, 1875.

105. *Nashville Daily American*, July 3, 1916.

106. *Nashville Daily American*, April 22, 1876.

107. Ibid.

108. *Nashville Daily American*, April 20, 1884.

109. *Nashville Daily American*, May 21, 1880.

110. *Nashville Daily American*, June 15, 1878.

111. *Nashville Daily American*, November 11, 1876.

112. *Nashville Daily American*, October 24, 1877.

113. *Nashville Daily American*, June 16, 1877. See also: *Nashville Daily American*, June 8, 1877; June 17, 1877; June 23, 1877.

114. *Nashville Daily American*, June 16, 1877.

115. Langston Rifles took its name from John Mercer Langston, the great Black attorney, educator, activist and politician who personally presented the company with its colors in a ceremony at St. John's AME Church in Nashville. See: *Nashville Daily American*, December 6, 1885.

116. *Nashville Daily American*, July 29, 1879.

117. *Nashville Daily American*, February 13, 1889.

118. *Nashville Daily American*, July 22, 1883.

119. *Nashville Daily American*, August 20, 1886.

120. Ibid.

121. Ibid.

122. *Nashville Daily American*, January 2, 1890.

123. *Nashville Daily American*, July 5, 1890; July 7, 1890.

124. *Nashville Daily American*, July 8, 1890.

125. *Nashville Daily American*, July 9, 1890.

126. *Nashville Daily American*, January 17, 1898.

127. *Nashville Daily American*, February 28, 1882.

128. *Nashville Daily American*, June 1, 1875.

129. *Nashville Daily American*, June 19, 1877.

130. *Nashville Daily American*, May 26, 1888.

131. *Nashville Daily American*, July 18, 1889. A sham battle was likewise held in Nashville at the state competition in 1889.

132. *Nashville Daily American*, July 18, 1889; May 27, 1888.

133. Ibid.

134. *Report of Laps. D. McCord, Adjutant General of the State of Tennessee to His Excellency, Robt. L. Taylor, Governor, December 31, 1888* (Nashville, TN: Marshall & Bruce, Printers, 1889), 3.

135. *Nashville Daily American*, January 27, 1888.

136. Ibid.

137. Ibid.; *Nashville Daily American*, February 13, 1889.

138. *Nashville Daily American*, January 27, 1888.

139. *Nashville Daily American*, November 3, 1900; July 6, 1901; August 21, 1901; May 27, 1905; January 11, 1906; September 24, 1909; February 23, 1913; August 28, 1917; *Nashville Tennessean*, June 10, 1907. The men of the Porter Rifles offered to serve with American forces in the war to make the world safe for democracy, but their zeal was outweighed by their advanced years.

140. *Nashville Tennessean and the Nashville American*, April 18, 1917.

## Chapter 4

141. *Nashville American*, April 12, 1896.

142. *Nashville Daily American*, June 15, 1883.

143. *Nashville Daily American*, July 30, 1883.

144. *Nashville Daily American*, July 1, 1888.

145. *Nashville Daily American*, August 4, 1889.

146. Ibid.

147. Ibid.

148. Ibid.

149. *Nashville Daily American*, April 12, 1896.

150. Ibid.

151. *Nashville Daily American*, July 1, 1888.

152. One who sped dangerously to excess.

153. This sort of extreme exercise results in the increase of endorphins, hormones related to a sense of well-being. This was not known in the nineteenth century.

154. *Nashville American*, July 1, 1888.

155. *Nashville Daily American*, May 11, 1896; Wikipedia, "Good Roads Movement," en.wikipedia.org/wild/Good_Roads_Movement. See also: *Nashville American*, January 27, 1889; June 23, 1889; February 12, 1897; February 10, 1898.

156. *Nashville American*, January 27, 1889.

157. *Nashville American*, December 9, 1888.

158. *Nashville American*, January 13, 1889.

159. *Nashville American*, July 1, 1888.

160. *Nashville American*, June 29, 1888.

161. *Nashville American*, July 2, 1889. El Dorado cannot be identified. It may have been a nearby spa in Davidson County; *Nashville American*, July 14, 23, 1887; see also: *Nashville American*, November 25, 1888. A cyclometer was analogous to an odometer.

162. *Nashville American*, July 14, 1887.

163. Emphasis added.

164. *Nashville American*, June 29, 1888.

165. *Nashville American*, May 26, 1889.

166. *Nashville American*, June 9, 1889.

167. *Nashville American*, September 21, 1888.

168. Ibid.

169. *Nashville American*, September 22, 1888.

170. Ibid.

171. *Nashville American*, July 2, 1888.

172. *Nashville American*, November 11, 1888.

173. *Nashville American*, May 11, 1898.

174. *Nashville American*, October 31, 1895.

175. *Nashville American*, August 25, 1895.

176. *Nashville American*, April 12, 1896.

177. Goodreads, "Susan B. Anthony Quotes," http://www.goodreads.com/author/quotes/ 59711.Susan_B_Anthony.

178. *Nashville American*, July 1, 1888.

179. *Nashville American*, August 25, 1895.

180. *Nashville American*, October 7, 1888.

181. Most likely a safety.

182. *Nashville American*, July 28, 1889.

183. *Nashville American*, June 21, 1891.

184. *Nashville American*, March 27, 1892.

185. *Nashville American*, April 2, 1894.

186. *Nashville American*, April 8, 1894.

187. *Nashville American*, May 5, 1895.

188. *Nashville American*, May 9, 1895.

189. *Nashville American*, June 29, 1895.

190. *Nashville American*, May 19, 1895.

191. *Nashville American*, July 29, 1895.

192. *Nashville American*, April 2, 1896.

193. *Nashville American*, April 12, 1896.

194. *Nashville American*, September 15, 1895.

195. *Nashville American*, October 21, 1888; July 8, 1891; July 10, 1891.

196. *Nashville American*, September 15, 1895.

197. Roni Sarig, "A History of Cycling Sports," http://www.netplaces.com/bicycle/bicyclin g-for-sport/a-history-of-cycling-sports.html.

198. *Nashville American*, July 7, 1891.

199. *Nashville American*, September 15, 1895.

200. Sarig, "History of Cycling Sports."

201. *Nashville American*, November 24, 1895.

202. *Nashville American*, September 15, 1895; March 14, 1897; October 31, 1897.

203. *Nashville American*, May 10, 1904. See also: *Nashville American*, November 24, 1895; April 27, 1896; May 10, 1896; June 12, 1896.

204. *Nashville American*, June 4, 1899; June 8, 1899; June 11, 1899; June 12, 1899; June 13, 1899; June 19, 1899; June 3, 1900; June 4, 1900.

## Chapter 6

205. *Nashville American*, October 20, 1895.

206. *Nashville American*, October 27, 1895.

207. *Nashville American*, October 25, 1895.

208. *Nashville American*, October 27, 1895.

209. *Nashville American*, October 30, 1895.

210. *Nashville American*, November 3, 1895.

211. *Nashville American*, November 9, 1895

212. *Nashville American*, December 5, 1897.

213. *Nashville American*, November 26, 1895.

214. *Nashville American*, November 11, 1897.

215. *Nashville American*, November 28, 1896; December 1, 1896; December 15, 1896; August 8, 1898; January 29, 1899; December 20, 1901; December 22, 1902; December 30, 1902; *Nashville Tennessean*, January 12, 1900.

216. *Nashville American*, December 30, 1902.

## Chapter 7

217. *Chattanooga Daily Times*, December 20, 1917.

218. *Chattanooga News*, January 15, 1918.

219. *Chattanooga Daily Times*, May 12, 1918.

220. *Nashville Tennessean*, August 30, 1918.

221. *Chattanooga News*, December 13, 1917; *Chattanooga Daily Times*, December 24, 1917.

222. *Chattanooga Daily Times*, December 16, 1917; *New York Times*, December 16, 1917.

223. *Chattanooga Daily Times*, December 24, 1917.

224. *Chattanooga News*, December 13, 1917; January 15, 1918; *Chattanooga Daily Times*, December 16, 1917; December 18, 1917; December 23, 1917; December 24, 1917; May 12, 1918; *Nashville Tennessean*, August 30, 1918; *New York Times*, December 16, 1917.

225. *Chattanooga Daily Times*, December 23, 1917.

226. *Chattanooga News*, December 13, 1917; January 15, 1918; *Chattanooga Daily Times*, December 16, 1917; December 18, 1917; December 23, 1917; December 24, 1917; May 12, 1918; *Nashville Tennessean*, August 30, 1918; *New York Times*, December 16, 1917.

227. *Chattanooga Daily Times*, December 24, 1917.

228. Ibid.

229. Ibid.

230. Ibid.

231. *Chattanooga Daily Times*, December 23, 1917.

232. *Chattanooga News*, December 13, 1917; January 15, 1918; *Chattanooga Daily Times*, December 16, 1917; December 18, 1917; December 23, 1917; December 24, 1917; May 12, 1918; *Nashville Tennessean*, August 30, 1918; *New York Times*, December 16, 1917.

233. *Chattanooga Daily Times*, December 25, 1917.

234. *New York Times*, December 25, 1917. See also: *Chattanooga News*, January 22, 1918.

235. *Chattanooga Daily Times*, December 25, 1917; December 26, 1917

236. *Chattanooga News*, January 2, 1918.

237. *Knoxville Journal and Tribune*, January 3, 1918.

238. *Chattanooga News*, January 8, 1918.

239. *Chattanooga News*, January 9, 1918.

240. *Chattanooga News*, January 15, 1918.

241. Ibid.

242. *Knoxville Journal and Tribune*, January 16, 1918.

243. *Chattanooga Daily Times*, January 18, 1918.

244. *Chattanooga News*, January 16, 1918.

245. *Chattanooga News*, January 17, 1917; January 18, 1917.

246. *Chattanooga Daily Times*, January 16, 1918; *Chattanooga News*, January 17, 1918.

247. *Knoxville Journal and Tribune*, January 17, 1918; January 18, 1918.

248. *Chattanooga Daily Times*, January 18, 1918; *Chattanooga News*, January 18, 1918.

249. Ibid.

250. *Chattanooga Daily Times*, January 19, 1918.

251. *Chattanooga News*, January 22, 1918.

252. Ibid.

253. Ibid.; *Chattanooga News*, January 28, 1918. See also: Harding Affair, "Cast of Characters," http://thehardingaffair.com/cast-of-characters/.

254. *New York Times*, February 28, 1918.

# ABOUT THE AUTHOR

*J*ames B. Jones holds a doctorate in history and historic preservation. He is the author of countless such publications as the *Tennessee Historical Quarterly*, the *Public Historian* and *Civil War History*. He is the winner of the West Tennessee Historical Society's Marshall T. Wingfield Award. He is the retired public historian for the Tennessee Historical Commission. He is the author of several books by The History Press.

*Visit us at*
www.historypress.com